Selection a
Assessment:

A NEW APPRAISAL

Mike Smith · Mike Gregg · Dick Andrews

Pitman

Pitman Publishing
128 Long Acre, London WC2E 9AN
A Division of Longman Group UK Limited

First published 1989

British Library Cataloguing in Publication Data
Smith, Mike, 1945 Jan. 24-
Selection and assessment.
1. Personel. Selection
I. Title II. Gregg, Mike III. Andrews, Dick
658'.3'112

ISBN 273 03114 7

Typeset by Avocet Robinson, Buckingham
Printed and bound in Great Britain

Contents

Foreword

There are plenty of good books about selection and some of them are very good indeed. So why have we produced yet another? The answer is quite simple. We felt that the existing books left a gap which needed to be filled. As we went about our work of teaching, consultancy, or directing a personnel function we were often asked to recommend a good book which provided a straightforward, basic introduction to recent developments in the field.

For example, we were once asked by a trainee personnel manager to recommend something he could read on Assessment Centres. On another occasion we were asked by an expatriot returning to the UK for a quick introduction on the latest developments in biodata techniques, and a colleague in clinical psychology who had last studied occupational psychology in the 1970s wanted a short, up-to-date summary on the latest thinking on bias in selection. In each of these cases we found it difficult to give an adequate response. There were plenty of books and plenty of reports and plenty of journals but short, jargon free and up-to-date accounts were much scarcer.

Our aim in writing the present volume was to produce something which would fill this gap. We wanted to cover most of the recent developments in a way which would highlight most of the modern developments and themes. A reader would then be able to follow up in subsequent reading those aspects most relevant to their purposes. Indeed, we would feel that further reading of this type is essential because in order to present a clear account of the main principles involved we have shorn our accounts of much qualifying detail.

Accordingly, most chapters end with either references or suggestions for further reading.

In writing we have tried to keep the needs of three groups of readers in our minds. First are the students of personnel management at an introductory level. Second are established personnel managers who, for one reason or another have not been able to keep up with latest developments via other channels. Third are psychologists from other areas such as clinical and educational psychology who once studied some selection and assessment and who now feel the need for an efficient update.

Mike Smith · Mike Gregg · Dick Andrews
May, 1989

1 New horizons in selection and assessment

The late 1960s view of selection and assessment

Twenty years ago many personnel managers had a very pessimistic view of personnel selection. This pessimism was based on two major considerations: the labour market and the scientific results obtained by psychologists. Many countries were experiencing full employment and there were skill shortages. Often employers were happy to accept most applicants in the mistaken belief that selection techniques in these market conditions were not worth the expense involved.

The scientific results obtained by psychologists provided no greater encouragement. Ghiselli, in the USA, started to collect the results of scientific studies of the accuracy of different methods of selection. By the mid 1960s it seemed that even the most sophisticated methods seemed to be fairly crude. The accuracy of selection is usually expressed in terms of a correlation coefficient and Ghiselli's results seemed to show that, on average, a good method would only produce a measly correlation of about 0.3.

To make matters even worse, these poor results seemed to be unstable. Studies would show that a test, for example, would give a correlation of 0.3 for one organisation but give a correlation of zero for another. The logical consequence was clear: different methods of selection should be checked in every separate situation where it was intended to use them. However, even if the expertise to do this were locally available, it would be a very costly business for apparently very poor returns.

Perhaps the final blow was the concern over equal

opportunities. New methods of selection attracted the attention of groups concerned about equality of opportunity. Many organisations reacted by retreating to traditional methods which, we now know, are less accurate and more prone to bias (see Chapter 8). One psychologist likened this to 'rats swimming towards a sinking ship'.

It seems understandable therefore that many personnel managers and psychologists threw up their hands in despair and decided to invest their energies elsewhere – in training, organisation development, morale studies and improving the quality of working life.

The hidden renaissance of the 70s and 80s

Despite this depressing scenario, academic work continued throughout the 1970s and early 1980s. By the mid 1980s most of this traditional thinking had been overturned and it now seems that proper selection of its staff is one of the best investments any organisation can make. But, unfortunately, many personnel managers remained unaware of the renaissance in the subject – largely because it is written up in technical journals and no concise, easily accessible account exists. The aim of this book is to remedy this situation.

The three pillars of the renaissance

The great change in the basis of modern selection and assessment is founded upon three main pillars.

- *First*, and most predictably, were the incremental changes to the technology which existed in the 1960s. Tests were improved, and new methods evolved. Essential infrastructure such as better job analysis and better development of criteria was developed. Many of these changes are described in other chapters of this book (see Chapters 2–7).
- *Second*, was an improvement in our understanding of the scientific methods we must use when evaluating selection systems. We learnt that many of the results collated by Ghiselli were fundamentally flawed. When these flaws were

corrected the accuracy of many methods of selection was much higher than we had suspected. Furthermore, research indicates that when these flaws are taken into account the accuracy of the different methods tends to be the same when it is used in different settings. These developments were absolutely crucial and will be dealt with in much greater detail in subsequent paragraphs of this chapter.

- *Third,* ways were established of working out the monetary value of selection. Utility theory enables personnel managers to face production managers, data processing and other managers squarely at annual budget meetings and argue their cases in the same money terms. Talking in terms of pounds, dollars, marks or francs is much more persuasive than talking in statistical terms such as correlations or 't' tests – especially since the results generally indicate that investment in selection procedures offers high rates of return to an organisation. Utility theory will be explained in more detail in Chapter 9.

The transformation from the depressing scene in the 1960s was made even clearer when, as Chapter 6 explains, doubts about the fairness of many methods were by careful analysis shown to be exaggerated.

Improvements in understanding the scientific basis of selection

Requirements of a perfect validity study

Studies of the accuracy of selection are usually termed validity studies and the requirements of a perfect validity study were established early in this century. In essence, a perfect validity study has four requirements:

- a large representative sample of applicants;
- measurement of each applicant by some method, such as an interview or a test, which results in a score on, say, a 1–10 scale;

- accurate measurement of each applicant's subsequent performance at work using, perhaps a 1–10 scale;
- relating the scores at selection to the subsequent performance at work. The simplest way of doing this is to draw a scattergram with the position of each applicant plotted using the selection score and the performance score. The scattergram can then be inspected to see if there is a clear trend which would indicate accurate selection. Unfortunately, the interpretation of the scattergram can be quite subjective since in dealing with human beings it is rare to see pure trends.

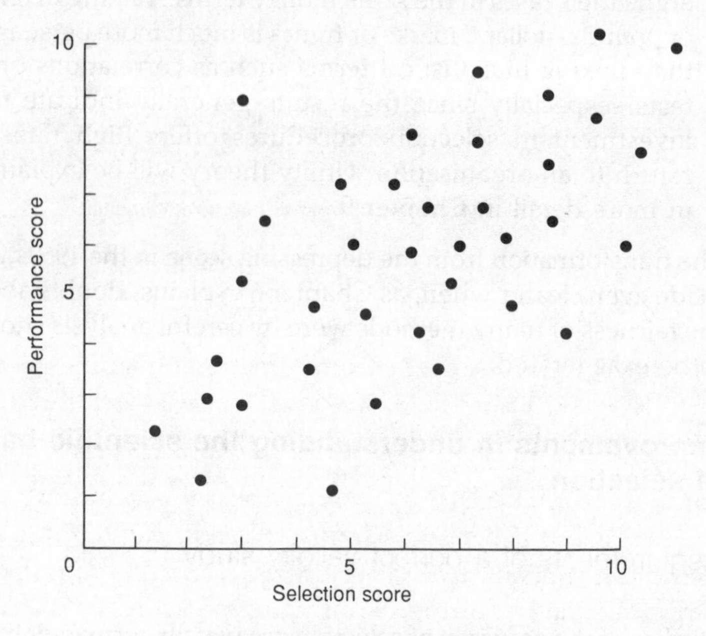

1.1 Scattergram from validation study

A better way is to calculate a statistical index which is unambiguous. Usually, the statistical index used in validity studies is the correlation coefficient. Correlations usually range from +1 indicating a perfect relationship between selection and performance and zero which indicates only a chance relationship. It is also possible to obtain negative correlations which indicate inverse relationships. In terms of validity, correlations may be interpreted as follows:

over 0.5	excellent
0.40 to 0.49	good
0.30 to 0.39	acceptable
less than 0.30	poor

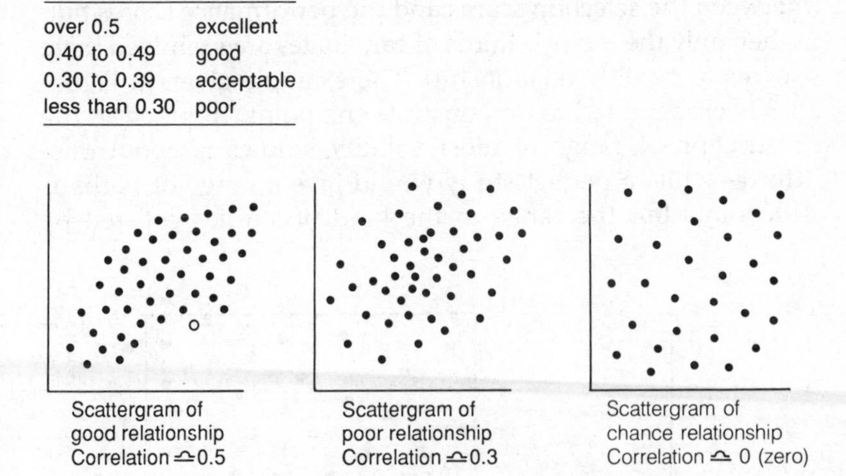

1.2 Scattergrams showing different relationships

Ghiselli's errors

During the 1950s and 1960s information on studies of these kinds was collected and it seemed that the validity of even the best methods of selection had only meagre validities of about 0.3. However, this conclusion often blindly assumed that the studies conformed to the ideal paradigm. As Frank Schmidt and Jack Hunter in the USA pointed out, often the studies contained two major errors: restriction of range and a contamination of the performance measures.

Restriction of range

An ideal validity study requires selection and performance information on *all applicants*. In practice, this is rarely achieved. Organisations often only hire those who pass a test or an interview. Consequently the two sets of information, the measures at selection and the measures of performance are only available for the top candidates. Restriction of range means that there is often not enough room for the trend to show. The effect is demonstrated in Figure 1.3. Looking at the figure as a whole, it is clear that there is a moderate relationship between the selection scores and the performance scores but, when only the top two-thirds of candidates are examined there seems to be little relationship. The example given in Figure 1.3 is exaggerated to demonstrate the point. In practice, the restriction of range in most validity studies is about one-third – while a perfect study would give a range of perhaps 10 points but the range in the kind of studies collated by

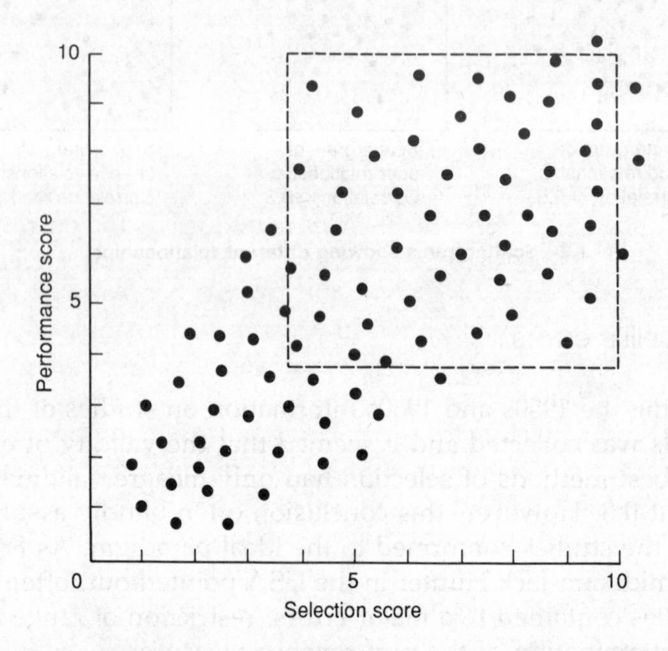

1.3 Diagram showing effects of restriction of range: when the whole range is examined a clear trend is discernible. When only the top ⅔ are examined the pattern appears random

Ghiselli would be about only six or seven. The usual effect of such range restriction is to underestimate the validity of selection. Fortunately, if other information is available, it is possible to use a statistical formula to calculate what the proper correlation should be.

Contamination of performance measures

The second source of error was more subtle: the performance data were wrongly assumed to be accurate. In many occupations, especially management and professional occupations, objective performance figures are not available and consequently investigators had asked the applicants' superiors to rate their performance on, say, a 10-point scale. However, it is abundantly clear that these ratings are not completely objective. If a superior is asked to give a second set of ratings after he or she has forgotten their initial ratings, there are often quite marked differences. These differences are usually even larger if the second set of ratings are produced independently by another superior.

The use of 'objective' performance information does not always help the situation. Sales figures for different salespeople are contaminated by factors over which the individual has no control, such as differences in sales territories or the current position in a trade cycle. Production figures for operatives, such as the number of units made, are also contaminated: some operatives may be working with better and newer equipment; some might be working with raw materials of better quality; some operatives may be working repetitively on one product while others have to cope with many changes of style which could involve continual adjustment and resetting of a machine.

It is clear, even from this very short discussion, that few performance measures are pure. Yet, early validity studies accepted these measures as 'given by God' and they attempted a naïve calibration of the selection methods against the impure criteria. It was like trying to calibrate a new ruler against a hand-drawn scale produced by craftsmen of a previous century: even if the new ruler were perfect it could never appear to be more than 60 per cent accurate because the scale against which it was judged was only 60 per cent accurate.

Impurities in the performance measures tend to further underestimate the accuracy of a selection method. Fortunately, again, given the right additional information it is possible to use statistical formulae to correct this underestimation. More recently, as Chapter 3 will show, psychologists have devoted much more care and attention to the criteria they use in validation studies.

Impact of small sample size

Most of the studies reported in the 1950s and 60s were based on a small sample size of about 60 applicants. Even today the average size of a validity study is only about 110. Researchers should not be criticised for this because in most organisations outside the armed forces or government it is rare to find more than 50 or 60 people doing the same job. However, the small sample size of many validity studies has important implications. Almost every introductory book on statistics emphasises that conclusions based on small samples are very unstable – simply because the laws of chance do not have room to cancel out random errors. A typical opinion poll would use a sample of over 1,000 people, yet psychologists were basing *their* conclusions on samples of less than 100 cases – no wonder they often obtained inconsistent results.

Indeed, it was realised by the mid 1970s that most of the situational specificity noted by Ghiselli and his colleagues was merely random sampling error. When large samples were available, methods of selection tended to produce the same results in different organisations and in broadly similar jobs.

However, the fact remains that most occupational samples are small. Fortunately, Hunter and his colleagues in the USA developed a technique called *meta-analysis*. Meta-analysis is a statistical technique which combines the results from many small studies to produce findings based on large samples. For practically the first time in their history, industrial psychologists were able to give authoritative estimates of the accuracy of different methods of selection. Some results, corrected for both restriction of range and contamination of the criteria, are given in Figure 1.4.

The figure must be interpreted with care because in summarising the points of meta-analyses to date some important details have been omitted. For example, we are more sure of some results than others: the positions of interviews,

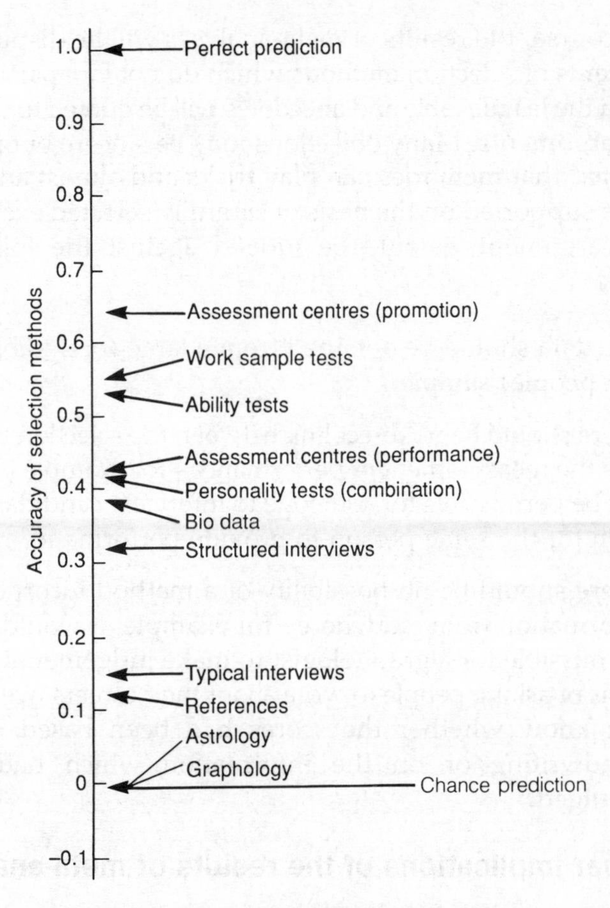

1.4 Accuracy of some methods of selection

work-sample tests and ability tests will be fairly accurate because they are based on thousands of cases. The position of personality tests is much less authoritative and it is based only on modern tests. Measures of personality such as clinical ratings and ink blot analysis have been excluded. It is also based on the best combination of scales contained in a test; the accuracy of any one part of a personality test is much poorer and, typically, a correlation of only 0.16 is obtained for a single score from a personality test, but when the most relevant scores are combined the accuracy of these tests seems much higher.

Of course, the results of meta-analyses will be disputed by adherents of selection methods which do not fare particularly well in the league table and anecdotes will be quoted to support their arguments. Many objections may be sincere but it must be noted that memories can play tricks and almost anything can be supported on the basis of carefully selected examples. Such arguments should be judged against the following criteria:

- The data should be obtained from a large (preferably over 200 people) sample.
- There should be no direct link between the selection method and the measurement of performance – for example it would not be permissible for someone to interview candidates and then for the same person to provide performance ratings.
- There should be no possibility of a method incorporating information from elsewhere – for example, it would not be permissible for a graphologist to make judgements on the basis of asking people to write about their careers: we would not know whether the scores had been based on the handwriting or on the information which had been divulged.

Further implications of the results of meta-analyses

One of the great advantages in the improvements of the last twenty years is that they have produced results of which we can be fairly confident. The results can be used to explore future horizons. For example, most meta-analyses suggest that cognitive ability tests (something similar to intelligence tests) tend to be one of the best predictors of subsequent job performance and this seems to be true for jobs at most levels. The question then arises, why is this so? The results from meta-analyses allow us to answer the question with some certainty. Cognitive ability helps us to do our jobs better because it helps us solve the problems we encounter in our work. However, that is not the main reason. It would seem that cognitive ability helps predict job performance because intelligent people find it easier to learn about the job and thus they have greater knowledge of what is involved. They are then able to draw upon this knowledge to deal with important situations rather than having to take time to solve the problem *de nouveau.* It is to be hoped that in due course further results of meta-analyses will be available which will help unravel the way in which personality influences job performance.

Another exciting possibility which meta-analysis opens up is the comparison of the effectiveness of different strategies which personnel managers might pursue. The statistical methods which have been applied to the selection process can, with a little modification be applied to other personnel interventions such as training, worker participation, job restructuring. The approach is relatively new but as the following list (derived by Hirsch) shows, tentative results are emerging.

INTERVENTION	CORRELATION
· training	0.30
· financial compensation	0.17
· work redesign	0.14
· organisational development	0.09
· appraisal and feedback	0.09
· supervisory methods	0.05
· work rescheduling	0.05
· goal setting	0.05
· management by objectives	0.00
· realistic job previews	−0.01

These early indications need to be taken with much caution and the costs of the different strategies must be taken into account. But, the possibilities are exciting. We are clearly moving towards a situation in which personnel managers will have clear information on which to base rational decisions about the deployment of resources at their command. In other words, we are clearly moving towards the horizon of scientific human resource management.

A short reading course on new horizons in selection and assessment

First, readers who are unfamiliar with the subject or who are returning to the subject after a number of years should consult a recent textbook on selection such as:

Smith, J.M. and Robertson, I.T. (1986) *The Theory and Practice of Systematic Staff Selection,* London, Macmillan.

or Landy, F.J. (1985) *Psychology of Work Behaviour,* Homewood, Illinois, Dorsey Press.

Next, they should consult key papers such as:

Hunter, J.E. and Schmidt, F.L. (1982) 'Fitting people to jobs: the impact of personnel selection on national productivity', in Dunnette, M.D. and Fleishman, E. (eds) *Human Performance and Productivity,* Hilsdale, New Jersey, Lawrence Erlbaum.

Schmidt, F.L., Hunter, J.E. and Urry, V.W. (1976) 'Statistical power in criterion-related validation studies', *Journal of Applied Psychology,* 61, **4**, 473–85.

Schmidt, F.L., Hunter, J.E. and Pearlman, K. (1981) 'Task differences as moderators of aptitude test validity in selection: a red herring', *Journal of Applied Psychology, 66,* **2**, 166–85.

Hunter, J.E. and Hunter, R. (1984) 'Validity and utility of alternate predictors of job performance'. *Psychological Bulletin,* 96, 72–98.

Hunter. J.E. and Schmidt F.L. (1989) 'Meta Analysis: Facts and Theories', in Smith, J.M. and Robertson, I.T. *Advances in Selection and Assessment,* Chichester, Wiley.

Finally they should consult the following books as background reading:

Ghiselli, E.E. (1966) *The Validity of Occupational Aptitude Tests,* New York, Wiley.

Glass, G.V., McGraw, B. and Smith, M.L. (1981) *Meta Analysis in Social Research,* Beverly Hills, Sage.

2 Recent strides in analysing jobs and attracting candidates

Job analysis

Job analysis is the cornerstone of good selection. As Figure 2.1 shows, it is the first stage in the whole selection process and everything else is built upon it. The effects of a mistake at this point are likely to ricochet throughout all subsequent stages. The growing realisation of the importance of job analysis is only partly due to an acceptance of the strategic position of job analysis. Many personnel managers now pay more attention to the subject because the courts in the USA tend to take the view that selection methods based on a proper job analysis are less likely to have an unfair bias against women and minority groups.

Traditional job analyses tend to be based on the tasks that make up the job and they are called *task-oriented analyses*. Typically, a task-oriented analysis consists of observing or interviewing a small sample of job incumbents and generating a list of activities they are required to perform. Sometimes this stage also involves discussions with the incumbent's superior. Usually, the next step in a traditional analysis is to cast the information into a questionnaire which is completed by a larger sample of incumbents who are asked to tick those activities which form part of their job. Sometimes, the incumbents will be asked to indicate how important a task is and how frequently it occurs. The end product of this traditional analysis is an ordered list of activities. The list will be of direct use in building selection systems based upon a sample of the job.

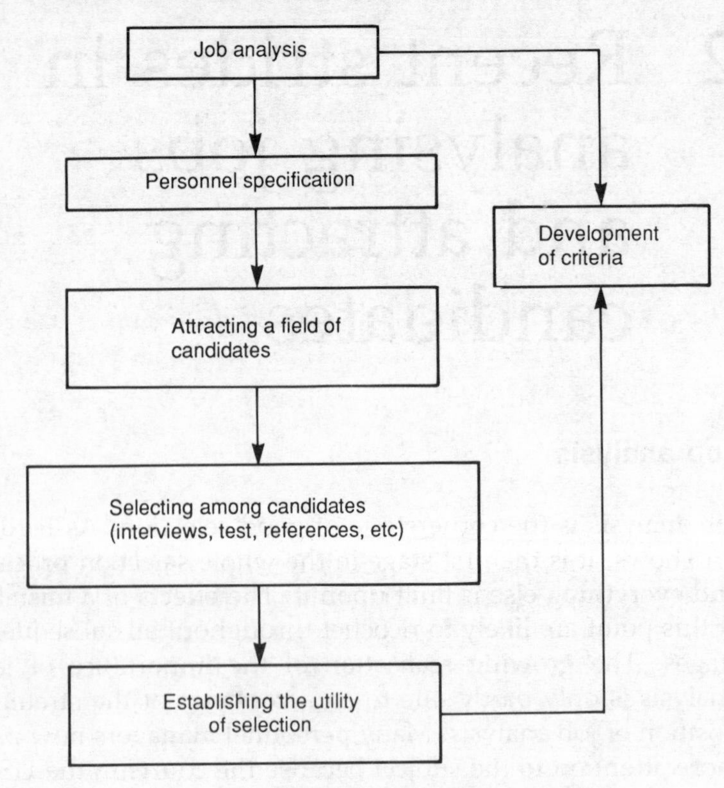

2.1 The selection paradigm

For example, if the analysis shows that tracing faults in a circuit board is the most frequent task then it would make sense to give applicants a mock-up of a simplified circuit board containing known mistakes and observe whether he or she is able to identify them.

Traditional analyses of this kind have been conducted over many years and are often very useful. But, they have two major disadvantages: specificity and skill 'blindness'. The analysis is usually couched in terms which are specific to that particular job. This makes it difficult to compare jobs which contain tasks that have unique names but which, in fact, are very similar to tasks in other jobs. Traditional analyses of tasks may also be unsatisfactory because most recruiters want to know about the skills they should seek from candidates in terms of such things as manual dexterity, spatial ability or resistance to stress. A part of the answer is to conduct a *worker-oriented job analysis* which focuses on the activities performed. For example, a worker-oriented job analysis would be couched in terms of 'adjusting precision optical equipment' or 'coping with complaints from "bounced" airline passengers'.

Comparisons between worker-oriented and task-oriented analyses have been inconclusive, with neither type proving to be consistently more useful than the other. However, both types have the disadvantage that they rarely go the whole way. The objective of a job analysis is to provide a basis for specifying the skills and qualities which are needed to perform a job. A statement of the tasks or the worker activities does not, on its own, provide this specification – the skills and qualities need to be inferred from the job description. Most methods of job analysis leave this crucial step up to the whims and intuition of the individual recruiter. There is very little evidence concerning either the reliability or the validity of such inferences. A poor inference concerning the skills and qualities needed can have important consequences for later stages.

For example, one company manufacturing equipment used by research chemists correctly identified 'customer contact' as an important task in the job of its sales force. From this they inferred that they should select fairly extroverted people and they included a test of extroversion in their selection procedure. A subsequent validity study revealed a low negative correlation (−0.1) between sales success and the test score. From this they concluded that personality tests were not valid and expunged them from all their selection procedures. Unfortunately, the company had made the wrong inference concerning the skills needed for the type of customer contact experienced by their sales force. Research chemists tend to be dry, logical and rather introverted customers. They were uninfluenced and perhaps slightly antagonised by the brash enthusiasm of an extroverted salesperson. The purchase was a substantial one and the research chemists were more interested in receiving data on the reliability of the equipment and how it would meet their requirements.

A competitor selling similar equipment made a different inference from its job analysis. It too concluded that the personality of the salesperson was likely to be important, but luckily it drew the right inferences and selected on the basis of imagination, experimental outlook and self-control. Their validity study produced a correlation of 0.43 between a combination of these characteristics and sales performance. The second organisation congratulated itself on its judgement. An independent observer would have had difficulty in distinguishing between their actions and thoughts and those of the first company. The success of the second company was largely a matter of luck.

The importance of this link between the job description and the personnel specification has been recognised and more systematic ways of making the link are being developed. In some methods such as repertory grid analysis the link between tasks and skills is an inherent part of the procedure. In other questionnaires, notably the PAQ and the WPS (see below), the link is provided by a series of weightings for each skill. The scores on the job analysis questionnaire are multiplied by the appropriate weighting to produce an estimate of how important the skill is to adequate job performance.

Questionnaires and check lists are often the most practical way of analysing a job. Producing questionnaires for these analyses can be tedious and time-consuming. Furthermore, it may involve specialist expertise which is not available to the organisation. Fortunately, a number of questionnaires have already been developed which can be used on many jobs without the necessity of developing 'tailor made' questionnaires. The main ones are listed below.

Position Analysis Questionnaire (PAQ) developed by McCormick at Lafayette University. This is probably the most widely used questionnaire and it contains about 150 scales. Each of these scales has specific examples (benchmarks) to indicate the level represented by the rating given. The PAQ is a worker-oriented questionnaire which can be completed by the incumbent, the incumbent's superior or a job analyst. One particular advantage of the PAQ is that the author has produced a set of weightings which can be applied to produce estimates of the skills needed.

The PAQ is a 'broad spectrum' job analysis questionnaire which is not particularly suited to the analysis of managerial or professional jobs. In recognition of this Mitchell and McCormick produced the *Professional and Managerial Position Questionnaire* which is similar in format to the PAQ but contains 98 scales and benchmarks which are relevant to managerial work.

Occupational Analysis Inventory (OAI) developed by Cunningham in North Carolina is an inventory containing 622 descriptions of work activities and work conditions which are grouped into five categories: information received, mental activities, observable behaviour, work outcomes and work context. It was designed to achieve specific descriptions of jobs but it is applicable to the general population of jobs. The OAI is particularly good at capturing the technical content of jobs but it is also time-consuming to use.

Job Components Inventory (JCI) was developed in Sheffield by Banks *et al.* and it contains almost 400 items covering tools and equipment, physical and perceptual requirements, mathematical requirements, and decision making and responsibility. It is particularly strong in the areas of mathematical requirements and tools and equipment. Analysis takes the form of an interview with the incumbent and it lasts about 45 minutes. The psychometric properties of the scale are good.

Functional Job Analysis (FJA) was developed by Sydney Fine. It is not so much a questionnaire but more a method of analysing jobs using a controlled vocabulary. Several days' training in the technique is needed.

The **Knowledge, Skills, Abilities and Other Personal Characteristics Approach** was developed by Levine. It attempts to characterise tasks in terms of the time they occupy, their difficulty and the consequences of error. This too is not so much a standard questionnaire as a method of analysing jobs. Sometimes this is referred to as C-Jam (Complete Job Analysis Method) or B-Jam (Brief Job Analysis Method).

A very recent development has been the work by the Saville Holdsworth organisation on the **Work Profiling System.** The system is very professionally produced. A pilot investigation using a sample of 53 respondents indicated that it was easy to read and understand and that it gave a comprehensive view of the job. The system takes the form of three interlocking questionnaires suitable for:

- Managerial and professional workers
- Service and administrative workers
- Manual and technical workers

One advantage of this sectionalisation is that, although the total item pool is about 800, any individual will be faced with only 300–400 of the most relevant ones. This reduction can be carried a stage further because the items are grouped into sections around a common theme and there is a system for choosing the eight or more sections which are the most relevant for the job under analysis. Each of the questionnaires is divided into two parts. The first part is devoted to job tasks which are couched in worker-oriented terms and the analyst is asked to estimate both the time spent on each task and the importance of each task. The second part asks about the context of the job and collects data on such things as the physical environment, organisational size and job autonomy.

The Work Profiling System takes about 50 minutes to complete and it yields so much information that computer analysis of the optical scanning answer sheet is almost essential. The computer-generated report gives results in terms of 32 generic activities such as 'planning' as well as results for the individual components of these activities such as 'setting short-term objectives', 'planning a logical sequence' or 'anticipating problems'. A typical report on a management job would occupy 17 pages.

The final stage of the Work Profiling System is to transform the results of the job analysis into a personnel specification which details the characteristics of the ideal person for the job.

As noted above, this crucial step is usually ignored by most job analysis systems. However, the Work Profiling System provides a facility of deducing these attributes on a reasonably objective basis. Thus the system attempts to predict the job's requirements for up to 199 human characteristics such as hearing, generating creative ideas and confident communication. These predictions are obtained by weighting each of the responses to the first part of the WPS in a certain way. Ideally, these weights should be established empirically by measuring the relationship between a task and the different human qualities. Unfortunately, the WPS has substituted weights estimated by its in-house consultants for empirically determined weights. In ideal terms this must be considered a weakness of the system but in relative terms it must be considered an advance: most other systems simply ignore the issue and leave the deduction of human characteristics from job descriptions to the analysts' unguided intuition. A typical report on the human attributes needed to perform the job would be about nine pages long.

One final feature of the Work Profiling System which differentiates it from all other job analysis systems is that an attempt is made to make the next link between the characteristics needed to perform a job and the choice of selection method to measure these characteristics. For example, if planning is a significant aspect of a job the WPS produces a number of questions concerning planning which could be asked at an interview. Furthermore, the system also suggests the tests or other measures which are relevant to the skills needed.

One of the difficulties with most of the existing methods is that they merely focus on one aspect of job analysis – usually the tasks but sometimes the skills involved in the job. One relatively new approach is **Repertory Grid Job Analysis (RGJA).** Repertory Grid Job Analysis starts with a list of, say, 20 tasks which have been obtained in some way such as a previous survey or a list devised by a committee of 'experts'. Lists of this kind are available in most organisations and they can usually be provided with relatively little effort. The skills needed to execute the tasks are then elicited from the person doing the job or from a sample of people who can be reasonably expected to know the job well.

The elicitation procedure is fairly straightforward. Three of the tasks are chosen at random and the people providing information about the job are asked which one task is the odd task out in terms of the skills that are involved. The actual nomination is not important. What is important is the reply to the next question – 'Why, in terms of skills and abilities, is it the odd one out?'. The reason is noted and the process is repeated with other random triads of tasks until no new reasons are given. It is important to note that this approach does not place any constraints on the answers a person may give – they can answer in any frame of reference they like: consequently, rich and unexpected data can be produced.

At the end of this stage a list of tasks and a list of relevant skills have been produced and, depending upon the exact design and circumstances, they will be based on an individual incumbent or sample. The lists are useful information in themselves and many analysts are content to stop here. However, a proper repertory grid analysis will involve two extra stages: ratings and analysis. The ratings are obtained by taking each skill and giving each task a grading on, say, a seven-point scale according to how much of that particular skill is involved. This is then repeated for all the other skills which have been elicited. The rating process is usually, but not necessarily, achieved most economically by casting the data into a grid with the tasks along the top and the skills down the side as shown in Figure 2.2.

The grid of numbers contains a great deal of quantitative information about the tasks, the skills and the relationships between the two and this information is best analysed with a computer program – usually Patrick Slater's grid analysis package (GAP). Among other things, the package conducts a principle component analysis which scans the grid looking for an underlying trend. When it has located the trend the computer calculates its strength and then subtracts the effects of the trend from the grid. The program then looks for another trend in what remains. This process is repeated until all the

Tasks

7 A very high level of this skill is essential for the task
6
5
4
3
2
1 The task does not involve this skill

Skills	Understanding policy	Measuring performance	Lecturing	Appearing before PAC	Working on cabinet papers	etc
Ability to express viewpoint	2	1	5	7	3	
Ability to assemble facts	5	5	3	6	4	
Using Gantt charts	1	2	1	1	1	
Ability to talk convincingly	1	1	6	6	2	
Producing action plans	6	1	3	1	2	
Ability to motivate staff	1	5	4	1	3	
etc						
etc						

2.2 Example of repertory grid in job analysis

information has been extracted from the grid. At the end of this process there is a quantified list of the basic skills in a job together with a comprehensive analysis of how much each task is loaded with each basic skill. Further refinements mean that a diagrammatic representation of the job can be constructed with similar tasks clustered together.

A specific example should help to make the process and the advantages clearer. Some years ago, the Cabinet Office wished to analyse the job of top grade civil servants. An existing analysis which provided a list of the tasks undertaken by top civil servants and how frequently they occurred was quickly located. Typical tasks were: motivating staff, allocating priorities to work, producing written materials to ministers, supporting ministers before a select committee etc., etc. The 26 most frequently occurring tasks were selected for inclusion in the analysis. The skills needed to perform these tasks were then elicited from 19 top civil servants who also graded each task on each skill using a 7-point scale (7=skill essential to the task, 1 = task can be performed without the skill). The analysis revealed that according to the data provided by the 19 top civil servants, the most difficult *tasks* were:

	Index score
· Oral presentations and briefings to ministers	147
· Appearing before a select committee or PAC	128
· Planning the implementation of policies	117
· Supporting ministers or HoD before a select committee, etc.	103

Clearly, having a quantified list of this kind is very helpful in understanding the requirements of a job even though the index score should not be interpreted too literally. It enables the difficult, average, and easy tasks to be identified with precision and this in turn enables selection procedures and training methods to be more focused.

The principal component analysis revealed that there were eight significant trends in the *skills* needed:

1 Analytical ability	23%
2 Oral presentation skills	16%
3 Management skills	9%
4 Detailed specialist knowledge	6%
5 Drafting skills	5%
6 Decision-making skills	4%
7 Breadth of mind	4%
8 Foresight	3%
Miscellaneous skills	30%

A table of this kind should be of enormous help in constructing a selection system. As an unjustifiably crude example, the information suggests that, all other things being equal, if 10 hrs are available for the selection procedure, 2.5 hrs should be spent gauging analytical ability, 1.5 hrs should be spent assessing oral presentation skills, and so on. The table of loadings that accompanies the principal component analysis is also useful in breaking down individual tasks into the component skills. For example, in this case it was possible to show that oral presentations or briefings to ministers were difficult tasks because they had high loadings on trends 1, 2 and 4 (analysis, presentation and specialist knowledge).

The final refinement was to draw a diagram of the job as shown in Figure 2.3. In this diagram the tasks are located according to their positions on the first two trends and the tasks are clustered according to their overall similarity to each other.

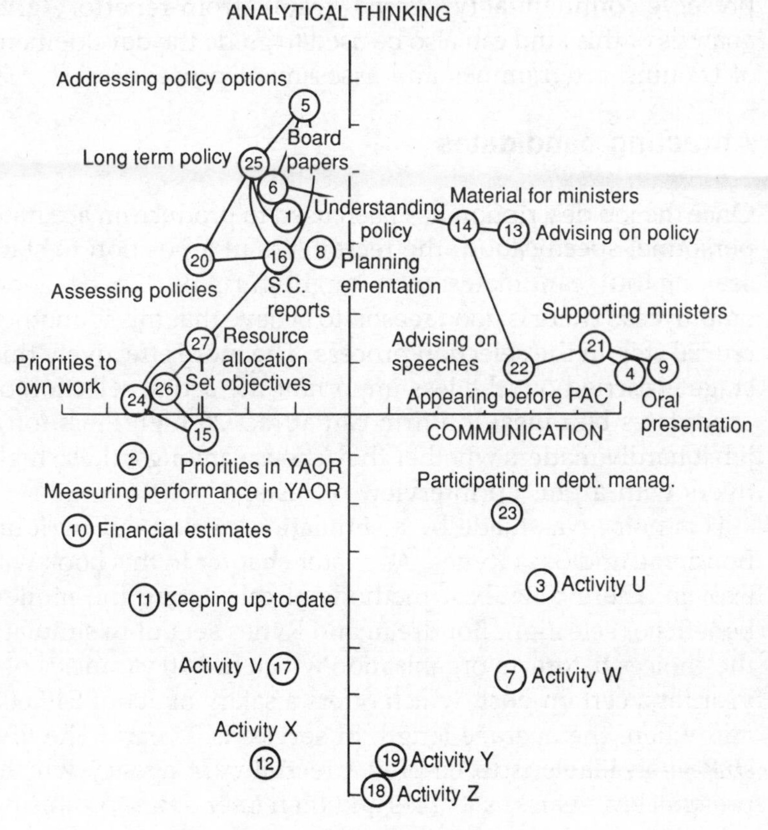

2.3 Analysis of job of senior civil servant

It can be seen that the job of a top civil servant consists of three large groups of tasks plus a number of unique tasks. The three clusters are: dealing with ministers, dealing with policy, and managing their 'department'. The diagram also has clear implications for the design of a selection system. For example, substantial effort would be justified in measuring each of the three major clusters – perhaps a role play of dealing with ministers, an analysis of a 'policy file' resulting in a written position paper and a simulation of managing and prioritising work in a department. The other individual tasks could be dealt with less intensively, say, at a situational interview.

There are two additional points worthy of note. *First,* this brief description has been amended and abridged in order to preserve confidentiality. *Second,* results from repertory grid analysis of this kind can also be used to guide the development of training programmes and assessment procedures.

Attracting candidates

Once the job description has been used to produce an accurate personnel specification, the recruiter is in a position to start seeking out candidates who might turn out to be good employees. There is good reason to believe that this is another crucial step in the selection process. The more effectively this stage is carried out the less important the actual selection of candidates becomes: if a firm can attract 20 high fliers for a job it hardly matters whether they choose amongst these high flyers with a pin, an interview or tests.

This point was made by a simulation carried out by John Boudreau and Sara Rynes. As a later chapter in this book will explain, there now exist methods of calculating the money benefits of selection. Boudreau and Rynes set out to simulate the choices before an organisation which has 10 vacancies per year for a certain post, which offers a salary of about $40,000 and where the average length of service is 2 years. The *first strategy* available is to employ a recruitment agency which, presumably, searches its files and then interviews 'promising possibilities'. The available research suggests that this strategy involves locating a fairly able pool of individuals, but selecting among these individuals quite inefficiently. The *second strategy* is to advertise in a newspaper and then use a fairly rigorous system of scoring the application forms and CVs. Research suggests that this strategy involves locating an average pool of individuals but then choosing amongst them more rigorously.

The question is, taking a 10-year view, which would be the best strategy? Boudreau and Rynes' calculations show that the first strategy would save the company $1,231,452, whilst the second strategy would save the company $706,406 – a difference of more than half a million dollars. This simulation, like all simulations, has its limitations but it does highlight two points. First, the better the recruitment the more difficult selection becomes and probably the best combination is the one which was not simulated by Boudreau and Rynes – good recruitment *and* good selection. Second, the recruitment strategy and its ability to locate a good pool of candidates is of vital importance to the ultimate cash value of the selection system.

Most recruiters will readily accept the last conclusion and will hasten to add the following question: 'Tell me which recruitment strategies work best'. There is a huge reservoir of anecdotal evidence because many recruiters have their own favourites. A survey by the British Institute of Management and the Institute of Personnel Management in 1980 revealed the following pattern of satisfaction with differing recruitment sources:

Method	*Satisfaction (1–5 scale)*
Internal recruitment	4.1
Local press	3.7
National press	3.5
Trade journals	3.2
Selection consultants	2.8
Private agencies	2.7
Head hunters	2.5
Government agencies	2.2
Professional registers	1.9

The survey also revealed that the local press scored highly in terms of cost effectiveness and speed while the trade press scored in terms of suitability of applicants. These results provide an interesting and probably accurate picture of what companies *think* about the recruitment media. They do not answer the central question concerning which media are the most effective in actual fact. It is noticeable that the satisfaction ratings in the list are directly related to the involvement of the company itself – a cynic would say that they are merely self satisfaction ratings.

What is needed is some scientific and dispassionate evidence. Unfortunately, little scientific evidence is available. It is an area of selection which has been greatly ignored. Furthermore, the evidence which is available tends to be self cancelling and is a matter of one step forward, one step backwards.

In the early 1970s there seemed to be some evidence that certain media were better than others. In particular it seemed that informal methods of recruitment such as self referral or referral by friends and relatives tended to produce a better quality of applicant – especially in terms of those who would stay with the organisation for a longer than average tenure. As the same result was found in a number of investigations various hypotheses were put forward to explain why it occurred.

The first of these hypotheses was the 'better waters' hypothesis. It was suggested that the different recruitment methods fished in different waters and that some waters contained a better quality of fish than others. Presumably, according to this hypothesis, the best people do not reply to newspaper ads or make themselves known to recruitment agencies: rather they speak up for themselves or their friends and relatives speak up for them.

The second hypothesis was the 'better info' hypothesis. It was argued that people who were suggested by other employees or relatives were better and more realistically informed about the job than those who applied through newspapers and agencies. Thus they were in a better position to assess their own suitability and perhaps the least suitable did not bother to apply at all. Consequently the average 'quality' of informally referred applicant tends to be higher. Better information might also influence labour turnover. Better informed candidates are likely to have a more realistic view of the job and consequently they would be less likely to leave when faced with the job itself. It is arguable that candidates from informal sources have discussed the job with the person who recommends them and that the job has been accurately described – warts and all. Candidates replying to newspapers, on the other hand, were probably obtaining their information from glossy brochures produced by the company's public relations department. When the actual experience of the job failed to match up to the high expectations a substantial proportion of recently appointed employees would find employment elsewhere.

The 'better info' hypothesis fitted in beautifully with the *zeitgeist* of the time. Work in progress in the USA was showing that labour turnover among candidates who were given realistic job previews of the job (RJPs) was lower. More recent research has cast some doubt upon the effectiveness of RJPs. Some reviewers have concluded that RJPs have little impact on turnover whilst other researchers suggest that a Realistic Job Preview only works when it is based on first-hand experience rather than a film or demonstration.

The third hypothesis to explain the apparent finding that informal sources of recruits produced a better quality of employee, is the 'cynic's' hypothesis. This contends that the result is little more than a self-fulfilling prophesy. Some studies used ratings by the supervisor as their measure of employee quality. Unfortunately, supervisory ratings can be notoriously subjective. Supervisors usually know how an employee has applied and many supervisors firmly believe in the importance of local knowledge and personal contact. Perhaps subconsciously they had allowed their feelings and knowledge to affect the ratings they gave.

However, all this speculation proved unnecessary because the scientific validity of the finding that informal sources produced better candidates fell into doubt. Some of the early studies had failed to control for the effects of seniority and tenure and they had lumped together jobs of different kinds. Older employees tend to stay with an employer for longer. There is also a tendency for informal methods to be used with senior positions. Consequently, when all types of jobs are mixed together in an investigtion an illusion is created. Recent work which has carefully controlled age and job level has failed to replicate the findings of ten years ago. It does seem to be a case of one step forward and one step back, but this should not daunt us in further work on the effectiveness of different recruitment media. It remains an area where a lot is opined but little is known.

Fairness in job analysis and in attracting candidates

It is apposite to end this chapter on a cautionary note. Thoughtless job analysis and thoughtless use of media can lead to illegal discrimination against women and minority groups. For example, poor methods of job analysis could lead to a personnel specification which artificially eliminates people who adequately perform the work. A classic situation has been described by Michael Pearn. An existing job analysis in one police force in the USA laid down minimum heights for police officers. Since men tend to be taller than women this height limit worked against women. Subsequent job analyses showed that the crucial requirement was, apparently, the ability to fire a revolver across the roof of a police car and that people several inches shorter than minimum height limit could achieve the task quite satisfactorily. The height limit was subsequently lowered. The limit still excluded more women than men but it was not held to be discriminatory since there was a demonstrable connection between the height specified and the ability to perform the duties of the job.

Recruitment methods may also have an impact on fairness. Most people will recognise the unfairness of advertising posts in magazines such as *Playboy* where, presumably, they are less likely to be seen by women and members of minority groups. Similarly, blatant bias in the wording of job advertisements is easy to recognise.

However, sometimes the effects are quite subtle. For example, one Midlands manufacturer genuinely believed that its recruitment methods were fair to all ethnic groups. It had a good reputation as an employer and a substantial proportion of its openings were filled by recommendations from existing and past employees. On closer investigation this informal system was found to be discriminatory because the ethnic groups were relatively new to the area and had not become a part of the informal network.

References

Banks, M.H., Jackson, P.R., Stafford, E.M. and Warr, P.B. (1982) *The Job Component Inventory Mark II: Training Studies,* Sheffield, Manpower Services Commission.

Cunningham, J.W., Boese, R.R., Neeb, R.W. and Pass, J.J. (1983) 'Systematically derived work dimensions: Factor analysis of the Occupation Analysis Inventory', *Journal of Applied Psychology,* **68**, 232–52.

Fine, S.A. and Wiley, W.W. (1971) *An Introduction to Functional Job Analysis: A scaling of selected tasks from the social welfare field,* Washington, DC, Upjohn Institute for Employment Research.

McCormick, E.J., Jeanneret, R.C. and Mecham, R.C. (1969) *Position Analysis Questionnaire,* West Lafayette, Indiana, Purdue Research Foundation.

Saville Holdsworth Ltd. (1988) *WPS Manual,* Esher, Surrey, Saville Holdsworth.

Smith, J.M. (1986) 'A Repertory Grid Analysis of supervisory jobs', *International Review of Applied Psychology,* **35**, 501–12.

Further reading

Probably the best single source of information on job analysis is:

Fleishman, E.A. and Quaintance, M.K. (1984) *Taxonomies of Human Performance,* Orlando, Florida, Academic Press.

A more colloquial book is:

Levine, E.L. (1983) *Everything You Always Wanted To Know about Job Analysis,* Tampa, Florida, Mariner Publishing Company Ltd.

3 Criteria for selection

All of us in the business of selection and assessment are also in the business of prediction. Whether we are personnel practitioners making judgements about people who might succeed in our organisation or external consultants advising companies about people they should or should not appoint, we are making predictions about likely success. So, what are we trying to predict?

At one level the answer is obvious and simple – successful job performance. It is only when we come to think about what we mean by successful job performance that the issue becomes more complex. Does successful job performance mean making profits for the company? Does it mean achieving a particular level of production or level of sales? Or does it mean motivating the sales force to achieve their quota? And if it does mean the latter, does it mean selling to existing customers or generating new business?

Questions such as these illustrate the difficulty surrounding the concept of criteria. They also help to explain why practitioners often gloss over the problem and instead concentrate on the methods or systems of selection and assessment.

The trap, of course, is obvious. How can we tell if our selection or assessment systems are accurate if we don't know what we are trying to predict? Put another way, how can we tell if we've hit the target if we don't even know what it is (let alone where it is)? This chapter looks at some of the issues involved in selection and assessment criteria and describes some new developments which may help us to tackle this thorny problem. We start with a definition.

What are criteria?

The Oxford Dictionary defines a criterion as 'a canon or standard by which anything is judged or estimated'. This canon or standard is generally taken to mean, in psychological research, a dependent or predicted variable for judging the effectiveness of anything from people themselves to the tests we use to select them – which still leaves us with a great deal of choice about what we mean by criteria.

To tackle this problem occupational psychologists have classified criteria in a number of ways. Two of the most popular are by type and by level.

Levels of criteria

One way of looking at criteria is to look at *job behaviours*. These are the behaviours we expect successful people to exhibit during the course of their job. For example, we may want managers to write clear reports or give interesting verbal presentations to groups of colleagues. These criteria are *immediate level criteria* and can be used to check whether people are conforming to expected behaviours, or can be used to judge the effectiveness of a test in selecting people who exhibit the required behaviours.

However, just because people can write clearly or speak well does not necessarily mean that they are being successful. Some organisations therefore look to the second level – that of results. A *results criterion* is something like a production level or a sales quota i.e. something that can be achieved by an employee. This level or criterion has the advantage that, if carefully chosen, the data on it are readily available and are objective or factual. Production data are often recorded on a weekly or even daily basis and sales data generally form the basis for salary commissions.

There are, of course, problems with using results level criteria. Often production levels or sales quotas are not entirely within the control of the employee. Machines break down, market demand for particular products changes, and some machines are just more efficient than others in producing a particular product. Using sales quota poses similar problems. One sales region might be 'easier' than another – it might be more densely populated, have higher income per head than others, or it might be geographically well placed to achieve sales targets. All these issues, which are beyond the control of individuals, contaminate the criterion we are using and it would therefore be inappropriate to judge people or selection systems solely by it.

The final level of criteria is that of the organisational level or the *ultimate criterion.* This level of criteria is concerned with how much an individual contributes to organisational goals. It is often termed the *dollar criterion* in that it has to do with the ultimate profitability of the company. But, how can we equate this with individual performance? If the results level is difficult to establish, the practicality of using organisational criteria for anyone, except perhaps the chief executive, must be questioned.

Types of criteria

Another way of classifying criteria is by *type.* Criteria can be either 'hard' or 'soft'. Hard criteria are from a family of criteria which concern *factual* data usually kept by an organisation or individual. These criteria have the advantage that they are *objective* and largely indisputable. For example, if sales per month are used as a criterion of success these are generally formally recorded and are open to inspection. The same is true of units of output, either per hour, per day or per week.

Soft criteria are, on the other hand, judgemental. They are criteria which come directly from the judgements of others – usually an individual's superior, although more recently some use has been made of self, peer and even subordinate ratings.

Hard criteria

Despite their objectivity hard criteria do have disadvantages and are much less used than they might be. Even though they are factual they are influenced by a number of *situational* factors, often outside the control of individuals. To demonstrate this let us look at some of the most popular hard criteria.

Absences

This is an important criterion because high degrees of absence adversely affect the performance of the organisation, especially when it is unauthorised or irregular. Managers are often reticent to hire individuals who are likely to be absent from work without good cause or who cannot be relied upon to turn up for work regularly. Unfortunately further analysis reveals the complexity of such criteria. A number of authors have reported that absence is related to job satisfaction, with dissatisfied workers being absent more often than satisfied workers. The size of the organisation is also an important factor, as is whether absence is paid or unpaid.

One of the most fundamental and dramatic measures of absence is voluntary turnover. If turnover is high, especially in the period immediately following selection, then it is reasonable to look at deficiencies in the selection system as a possible cause. Even this, however, has its problems. The general level of employment in the economy influences turnover. Low levels of unemployment and strong demand for labour increase turnover. Alternatively, turnover may not be due to a poor selection system. Induction may be faulty; training or supervision may be inadequate, or other factors such as working conditions may cause people to leave.

Indeed recent research has questioned the implicit assumption made in all criteria research that turnover is somehow bad. A recent review of meta-analytic studies (see Chapter 1) demonstrates that there is a strong correlation between job performance and turnover. The people who leave organisations are generally those whose job performance is worse than those who stay. Turnover, argue the authors, provides the organisation with the opportunity to replace poor performers with good performers. Providing that turnover is not a sign of an 'organisation in crisis', turnover can be positive rather than negative.

Accidents

In some jobs, e.g. production operatives, accidents may be an important criterion. After all, companies would not want to appoint individuals who are accident-prone. Nevertheless accidents are a poor criterion. To begin with most people have either one accident or no accidents in a year. This severely restricts the range of the criterion for use in testing a selection procedure. Furthermore, accidents are, by definition, outside the control of people, thus making them rather dubious as selection criteria.

Some efforts have been made to improve the use of accidents by focusing attention away from actual accidents to the observance of unsafe practices, but this moves away from 'hard' criteria towards judgemental, 'soft' criteria.

Production and sales

The use of production or sales data as success criteria has a great deal of attraction – especially in industries where they can be easily measured and collected. After all, output is what we require from all our employees, be it production operatives, secretaries, academics or managers. And, like all good criteria, the required information is readily available and generally easy to collect. This is even more so with the widespread use of computers. For example, secretarial output can be measured by sophisticated word processors which count and record the number of key-strokes. Computerised checkout systems at supermarkets measure the speed with which checkout operators process orders. Indeed the increasing use of technology may result in a renaissance in the use of hard criteria in both practice and research.

Smith and Robertson (1986) divide production criteria into three groups – quantity, e.g. units of output or sales per month; quality, e.g. percentage of rejects; and cost, e.g. cost per unit of production or cost per sale.

Despite their obvious attractions these criteria are often contaminated by influences outside the control of individuals. A secretary who keeps having to stop typing letters to answer phones, or a policeman whose clear up rate for crimes is slow because of lack of back-up facilities, or a badly trained production operative, can hardly be blamed for poor production figures. A similar picture emerges when sales criteria are used. A good sales territory will affect sales positively and a bad sales territory will depress sales, irrespective of the ability of individual salespeople.

Career progression

Career progression is sometimes used as a criterion. For example, speed of promotion and salary progression are sometimes used as criteria. But these too suffer from contamination effects. Speed of promotion may be a case of 'dead man's shoes', reorganisation, etc., and salary progression may be influenced by the external labour market, e.g. skill shortages or internal politics or policies, such as the desire of the organisation to ensure pay is in the top quartile.

Training

Success at training is often regarded as a good hard criterion. This is because it is less easily contaminated than some of the others mentioned. Trainees usually start at the same time, with the same facilities, and are given the same tuition. In addition the relatively short time periods involved in training mean that other influences, such as departmental politics and opportunities, have less influence.

The disadvantage with training as a criterion is, of course, inherent in its very nature. Once workers have been trained they are either classed as proficient or not. Thus, after a very short time period the training criterion is often reduced to a two-point scale and its use in validating predictors rapidly diminishes. In addition, the range of information about employee performance is necessarily restricted to the somewhat artificial environment of the training room. How this translates into actual job performance and the extent to which training covers the entire job domain are questions which cannot be answered by using training as the sole criterion.

'Hands-on' criteria

The difficulties with criteria contamination have made it very difficult to conclusively prove that predictors (e.g. tests) are related to criterion performance. This led Landy (1989) to develop what he called an ultimate 'hands-on', work sample criterion for the US military. Often used as predictors of performance, particularly in assessment centres, they have received little attention as criteria. According to Landy *et al.*, however, they do have a number of advantages when used as criterion measures. First, a 'hands-on' measure is a clear and definable part of a job, and second, it is administered in conditions that are standard and in which relevant behaviours which contribute to successful job performance can be observed. This reduces or even eliminates the problem of criterion contamination, and so makes the use of hard criteria much more attractive than they have been until now.

The major disadvantage, of course, with 'hands-on' criteria is cost. They are expensive to design and administer and because of this may be restricted to very large organisations or to the military where such costs may be somewhat more justifiable than in many other companies.

Despite their cost they should not be dismissed out of hand. When combined with the advances in technology the potential for using hard criteria looks better than it has ever done before.

Soft criteria

The problems associated with hard criteria have, at least until now, led researchers and practitioners alike to concentrate on soft or judgemental criteria. Research indicates that from over 500 validation studies carried out between 1914–1950 approximately 60 per cent used global ratings by superiors. This was supported by researchers in the 1970s who reported similar conclusions.

Readers, by now, will not be surprised to learn that ratings, too, have disadvantages. Ratings are prone to a number of systematic errors, the most important of which are summarised below.

- *Halo effect* This refers to the tendency of raters to transfer favourable or unfavourable assessments on one dimension to all other dimensions. For example, the manager who is rated highly on negotiating skills is also rated highly on interpersonal skills.
- *Leniency* Raters tend to give ratings which are skewed towards the top end of the scale. This reluctance to give poor ratings is a combination of at least two things. First, managers are unlikely to want to admit that they have underperforming people in their departments because it could reflect badly on their own ability to manage. Secondly, organisations often release the results to the people that have been rated. In this case, managers may want to avoid a dispute with the employees concerned and will certainly want to avoid demoralising them.
- *Central tendency* If raters do not skew their ratings favourably the chances are that they will use the middle points of the scale. This effectively reduces the variance around the mean score and therefore reduces any correlation between a predictor and the criterion.

These problems have resulted in a number of attempts to improve rating scales. One example is to represent a scale graphically thus:

Motivating others High ...x...x...x...x...x... Low

In this case the rater is asked merely to place a cross at the relevant point of the scale. Part of the problem with these trait type statements is, however, that they are very difficult to define. Motivating others to one person will mean being strong and directive while to another it will mean being democratic and participative.

Improvements can therefore be made by defining the trait description and by labelling the points on the scale, e.g. very high, moderately high, average etc. But even this leaves room for halo and leniency.

Probably the most sophisticated attempt to improve rating

scales has been made to two occupational psychologists, Smith and Kendall. They developed 'Behaviourally-Anchored Rating Scales' or BARS. They argued that it was lack of definition that caused most of the problems with ratings and suggested that if judgements were made on behaviours that could be observed many of the problems could be overcome. An ideal scale would therefore consist of two parts: (1) a clear definition of the trait to be rated, and (2) a description of the behaviours that could be observed at any level on a scale measuring that trait. An example of a BARS is given below.

High Performer	9 –	Identifies all customer needs; spots and acts on cross selling opportunities; can conduct all administrative procedures unsupervised
	8 –	
	7 –	Can conduct mortgage application interviews unsupervised and deal with relevant paperwork
	6 –	
	5 –	Can recommend appropriate services to known customer needs
	4 –	
	3 –	Can open and close savings accounts and complete necessary documentation
	2 –	
Low Performer	1 –	Cannot respond to the majority of customer needs without assistance

3.1 An example of a behaviourally anchored rating scale (for a building society clerk engaged in customer service)

BARS are formally constructed as follows. First, the key aspects of job performance are agreed upon, information which can often be directly transposed from the job analysis (see Chapter 2). Second, anchors are developed by asking supervisors to describe a number of 'critical incidents'. These are then sorted and assigned to each of the key aspects of job performance. Third, a panel of experts scale the incidents and an agreed rating scale is produced for each of the key job aspects.

Although BARS were initially enthusiastically received, more recent research is more sceptical. They are expensive to construct and are highly job specific.

Self and peer ratings

Although most ratings are of the 'boss' type, *peer ratings* have been used in some cases and have proved to be accurate predictors of performance against a number of criteria. They are cheap. Experts do not have to be employed to give assessments and the quantity of information available about an individual is greater than if only one boss rating has been completed.

However, they do suffer from two major disadvantages. They are unpopular and they require a long period of 'getting to know each other' before accurate ratings can be made. This latter problem restricts their use in selection and the former in assessing people for promotion.

These issues have effectively restricted the use of peer ratings to the armed services where groups of people live together for long periods of time and where peer assessment has a degree of acceptability. After all, an officer in charge of a platoon of soldiers may literally be responsible for their lives.

Self Assessment is more often used in industry, particularly as part of career development workshops (see Chapter 6). However, research has been much less conclusive than for peer assessments. Some studies report low correlations with job performance; others report higher correlations. Overall, the consensus of opinion seems to be that self assessment is much less useful than peer assessment. Primarily this is due to three main problems – leniency, reliability and hence validity.

Single or multiple criteria?

One of the most fascinating issues around at the present time is whether practitioners and researchers should use a single global criterion or use multiple criteria. It is interesting to see how opinions have changed.

Early research recommended the use of an overall indispensable criterion. However, later research doubted both the wisdom and practicality of such a single criterion. This change in view was based on the notion that in order to predict success one needs to know how it is made up. Dunnette (1976) argues that global criteria are over-simplified and misleading because job performance is a composite of many different elements. In addition, in most managerial jobs, a weakness in one area can be compensated for by strengths in others. Kingsbury (1933) put it succinctly when he said: 'Some executives are successful because they are good planners . . . others are splendid at co-ordination and direction, but their plans and programs are defective. Few executives are equally competent in both directions'.

This notion is supported by factor analytic studies such as Dunnette (1976). He identified four criterion factors in sales and technical jobs. These were initiative and persistence, personal commitment, knowledge utilisation and planning, organising and handling detail. Other research supports this view and evidence from job analyses carried out by the authors of this book suggests that most managerial jobs break down into at least five factors or skill/attribute groups.

Although factor analysis does produce more than one success criterion, recently the trend has once more reversed and the notion of a single global criterion has again gained ground. Much of this is due to the emergence of meta-analysis (Chapter 1). These studies question the need to discriminate among fine job criteria, particularly in selection, and suggest that a single global criterion of overall worth is as good as any other.

This approach would certainly make life easier for those responsible for selecting people into their organisations – but when should organisations use a global criterion and when should they use multiple criteria? Guion (1987) summarises the position as well as anyone when he quotes Patricia Smith who, at a conference in 1985, argued that the choice depends on the intended purpose. Guion summarises the position as follows:

> Her conclusion, using a military metaphor, was that you 'should use a rifle for small targets, a cannon for big ones, and a shot gun if you can't aim very well'.

Guion goes on to explain that the criterion used should meet the purpose for which it is needed. If specific problems need to be addressed, e.g. turnover, then specific criteria are needed. If overall measures of job performance are needed then a 'shotgun prescription' of a sample of the things that go to make up that successful performance should be combined to produce an overall, global measure of success. The key is to use the appropriate criterion for the problem at hand.

So, where are the new horizons in criteria? One must be that ratings continue to be the most popular form of criterion and that they are not as bad as we once thought. This conclusion is just one outcome of the meta-analytic work of the Hunter *et al.* group.

Second, and again as a result of meta-analytic studies, it seems that we don't *always* need to carry out local validation studies to validate predictors (particularly cognitive ability) (see Chapter 1). This is indeed a revolution because until a short time ago any self-respecting occupational psychologist would say that local validation must be conducted whenever tests or selection techniques were being considered. It follows from this that we generally don't need to discriminate among fine job criteria. In most cases, particularly for large-scale selection, overall job performance will be an adequate criterion.

Third, when we do need to conduct specific criterion research (e.g. for designing career development programmes) recent research has suggested that we don't need to rely exclusively on ratings. 'Hands-on' criteria can be considered and the increasing use of technology can make collecting data on 'hard criteria' much more reliable. Guion's (1987) view on the lack of progress of criterion research is, perhaps, a little too pessimistic.

Further reading

Dunnette, M. D. (1976) *Handbook of Industrial and Organisational Psychology*, Wiley.

Guion, R. M. (1987) 'Changing Views for Personnel Selection Research', *Personnel Psychology*, **4**, 199–213.

Landy, F. J. and Rastegary, H. 'Criteria for Selection', in Smith, J. M.

and Robertson, I. T. (eds) (1989) *Advances in Selection and Assessment*, Wiley, Chichester.
Smith, J. M. and Robertson, I. T. (1986) *Systematic Staff Selection*, MacMillan Press Ltd.

4 New light on an old friend: interviews

Changing views of the interview as a selection tool

Most people involved in selection and assessment will be aware that, for the most part, interviews have received a bad press. For years occupational psychologists have argued that interviews are among the worst methods of selection that organisations can use to choose its employees. As early as the 1920s Hollingworth described a study in which twelve sales managers came to remarkably different conclusions on who among 56 applicants were suitable for salesperson vacancies in their organisation. Many subsequent studies have given support to the view that interviews are bad at selecting the right people to do the job.

So, what is it about interviews that makes them so bad? To answer this question psychologists have assessed interviews against two main criteria – *reliability* and *validity*..

Reliability refers to either the extent to which the same interviewer would make the same judgement about, say, 20 candidates if he rated them twice in a given period of time (intra-rater reliability); or the extent to which different interviewers would agree on their ratings of a group of candidates (inter-rater reliability). Interviews are regarded as moderately reliable in terms of inter-rater reliability and reasonably good in terms of intra-rater reliability – although in this type of reliability memory and other complicating fractors (prejudice, bias) will influence the decisions made by an interviewer the second time around.

Validity refers to the extent to which interviews do what they are supposed to do, i.e. select 'good' candidates and reject 'bad' candidates. Unlike reliability, the statistics regarding the validity of interviews are pessimistic. Many researchers over the last 30 years have confirmed that interviews are very bad predictors of job performance. In other words, they are not a valid selection method. The reasons for this are many and varied. For example, research has shown that interviewers often make up their mind about a candidate in the first four or five minutes of an interview and then spend the rest of the time trying to justify their judgements. Second, memory seems to play a major part in an interview decision. Research on memory has concluded that people remember the information they get early and late in an interview (technically called the primacy/recency effect). They are less effective at recalling what goes on in the middle. For interviewers this means that they only use part of the information they get to make their decisions and that vital information (given in the middle of the interview) may well be overlooked and forgotten. Allied to this is the problem of concentration – most people have difficulty in concentrating for long periods of time. For interviewers, who may have to conduct five or six interviews in succession, concentrating all the time becomes impossible. The effect of this, of course, is that some information does not even get through to interviewers. Indeed, when the effects of lack of concentration and poor memory recall are combined the outlook for candidates does begin to look somewhat bleak!

Another problem with interviews is that different interviewers impose different standards on the interview. Some may be lenient and others may be tough; some may ask particularly difficult questions or questions which they hope will 'trip up' a candidate, while others may concentrate on 'easier' questions. In addition, the questions asked to elicit the information may vary widely. We can all recall somewhat odd questions by interviewers.

The somewhat arbitrary nature of questioning confirms that interviewers 'weight' the information they receive. For example, when faced with information about scholastic standing, business experience, and interests and abilities, research suggests that interviewers will place most emphasis on scholastic standing. Other research has found that interviewers weight any behaviour (good or bad) which seems to them to be out of the ordinary or unexpected. In addition, the interview is a social process and as such is sensitive to the effect of the behaviour of both interviewer and interviewee. This means that the interviewee can influence the outcome of the interview by using skills which do not necessarily equate with the skills needed in the job for which he or she is applying. Hollandsworth *et al.* (1979) describe three types of communication which can influence the outcome of interview decisions. These are verbal behaviour (what is said), non-verbal behaviour (actions and questions) and articulative behaviour (fluency of speech, loudness). Many researchers have shown that non-verbal and articulative behaviour are important influences on interviewers, although such behaviours may not necessarily give an indication of subsequent job performance.

So, if interviews have so many problems why do we use them? If they do not predict job performance very well should we not be replacing them with some other, more valid, techniques? Certainly there are many others ways of selecting employees, but it seems that, by and large, we still prefer interviews. In a survey from the *Times 1,000 Guide* Robertson and Makin (1986) reported that 99 per cent of all organisations used interviews at some stage in their selection process, and 96 per cent used references. This contrasted with the use of other techniques. For example, only 36 per cent of organisations used personality tests and only 30 per cent used some form of mental ability test.

Interviews, it seems, are here to stay – but why? Clearly, meeting candidates face to face is important. Employers must feel that candidates will 'fit-in' with their organisations before making a job offer. In addition, candidates must be given the opportunity to ask questions of their prospective employer because they, too, must be happy with the organisation and what it can offer, if they are to perform successfully in a job.

Given that interviews are an integral part of the selection process, there are a number of things employers can do to improve the performance of it as a selection tool. One can select interviewers, train them in interviewing techniques and give them a format to help them use effectively the information they get. All of these things will help to improve the power of the interview somewhat, but there are two improvements which seem to make a significant difference – structured interviews and panel interviews.

Structured interviews

Structuring an interview provides the interviewer with a *focus* on which to base questions and interpret replies. Essentially there are two types of structured interviews used in British industry. These are criterion-referenced interviews and situational interviews.

Criterion-referenced interviews are interviews in which candidates are asked specific questions designed to extract responses about their experience and/or skill in particular areas. These skills are established by a thorough job analysis (Chapter 2), and a standard set of questions or question areas is then designed to elicit information from the candidate on each skill. For example, if it has been established that communication skills are an important part of a job, an interviewer would ask questions such as:

'Can you describe an occasion when you gave a formal presentation to a group of people?'

'What were your objectives and to what extent did you meet them?'

'Why do you think you were successful (or unsuccessful) in meeting those objectives?'

The responses from the candidate would then be rated on a pre-determined scale such as a BARS (Chapter 2).

Situational interviewing takes a somewhat different approach. Typically, the method involves five stages:

First, the job is analysed using the critical incident approach. A sample of, say, 20 job incumbents are asked to nominate situations in their job which are typical of the job and which are crucial to success in the job. A consolidated list of these situations is produced and about 20 situations are selected for further development. The selection is mainly based on the frequency of occurrence but some may be included because they involve particularly important aspects of the job.

Second, responses to each of the 20 chosen situations are obtained. For example, the consolidated list will be sent to the job incumbents and they will be asked to give examples of a very good response which deals superbly with the situation, an average response and a poor response.

Third, the responses are then accurately scaled. For example, the best responses are sent back to the incumbents and this time they are asked to rate them on a 7-point scale. At this stage any responses which give rise to wide disagreement are eliminated.

Fourth, the situations and the scaled responses are collated into a booklet for use at the interview. The interviewer selects, say, six situations which are thought to be most appropriate. For example, an interview for salespeople to operate in a very competitive market might include the following situation:

You have made an appointment for an interview with a buyer of a major customer. When you arrive, you are kept waiting for 40 minutes without explanation. Just as you are about to get up and leave for your next appointment, the buyer emerges from his office in the company of a salesman from your competitors. What would you do?

Fifth, careful attention is paid to the candidate's reply and it is graded against the scaled replies produced at the end of stage three. For example, 'Blast the buyer for keeping me waiting and punch the other salesman on the nose', would obtain a poor evaluation. 'Explain that I was there on time and had been waiting and would try to arrange another appointment', would be an adequate response. 'Engage them in conversation and try to find out what they had been discussing before arranging a new appointment', would probably be given a good rating. At the end of the interview, the average rating for all the situations would be calculated.

Essentially, the difference between the two types of structured interviews lies in *where* the structure is focused. Criterion-referenced interviews focus on the characteristics or qualities of the applicant and as such deal in *signs*. Conceptually, they are similar to 'analytical tests'. Situational interviews, on the other hand, are akin to work samples or analogous tests. They deal in *samples* of work behaviour (see Chapter 6 for a detailed discussion of the differences between these types of test).

This difference makes the two types of interview useful in different circumstances. For example criterion-referenced interviews are probably better where candidates have little or no work experience (e.g. school leavers or graduates) or are external candidates who cannot relate to the activities of the specific jobs for which they are applying. Conversely, it is better to use situational interviews for applicants with some experience of the job in question – for example, internal applicants who are applying for promotion; or for external applicants with experience of the job for which they are applying – for example, an insurance agent from one company applying for a similar job in another.

Panel interviews

Panel interviews are popular in some organisations because they give more people the chance to assess a candidate. They have an intuitive appeal because they seem to be fairer on the candidate (since more than one person is involved in a decision) and they also spread the responsibility for making a decision among interviewers.

Panel interviews, however, do have disadvantages. They are probably more stressful than one-to-one interviews for the candidate and are both time-consuming and difficult to arrange for the organisation. Indeed, to overcome some of the problems some psychologists have suggested that panel interviews should be made up of three people – a chairperson, an internal specialist who has detailed knowledge of the job in question, and an outside specialist, such as a personnel professional, who can ask candidates about qualifications and experience in general terms.

New horizons in interviewing

There are two new horizons which will affect how managers and organisations will, or should, approach interviewing in the next decade. The first is the impact of meta-analytic research on the validity of interviews; and the second is the more practical problem of demographic change and how this will affect selection and assessment.

Meta-analysis

At the beginning of this chapter we suggested that interviews had, for years, been subject to a bad press and that the findings of occupational psychologists were consistent enough to be able to say confidently that interviews were among the worst predictors of job performance currently available. Meta-analysis has, however, placed this 'received wisdom' in doubt.

Weisner and Cronshaw (1988) conducted a meta-analysis on 150 validity co-efficients and concluded that, in fact, the interview was a much better selection instrument than the vast majority of psychologists were hitherto prepared to admit. Instead of reporting validity co-efficients of approximately 0.15 (as we might expect from previous research) they reported that a meta-analysis of previous studies raised the validity co-efficient to between 0.2 and 0.64, depending on the type of interview used.

Unstructured interviews, which probably constitute the vast majority of all interviews, still reported the lowest validity co-efficient (0.2), but structuring the interview, particularly by using a formal job analysis (Chapter 2) as a basis, increased the mean validity co-efficient by more than three times this figure to 0.63. However, what is also interesting about this research is that panel interviews did not seem to offer many advantages over individual interviews. *Provided the interview is structured*, individual interviews can predict performance just as well as panel interviews. On this basis organisations will undoubtedly be able to increase the performance of the interview as a selection tool without the expense of getting together panels. Overall, then, it appears that interviews still have a central place in the way we select our employees.

Demographic changes

Much of what we have said so far has assumed that the *power* of selection is in the hands of the employer: that the interview is used primarily to gain information from candidates and to use this information to assess his or her suitability for the job.

There is, however, another side to interviewing which hitherto has received little attention. That is the use of interviewing to *give* information to candidates. Indeed, apart from commenting that 'bad' interviewers talk too much, relatively little serious attention has been paid to the interview in this context. Demographic changes in the 1990s may lead us to change our view of this.

Demographic changes are likely to produce a shortage of suitably qualified people. Employers of graduates are likely to be particularly hit. The Association of Graduate Careers Advisory Services suggests that by 1999 the *supply* of graduates will be up by 4 per cent – but by 1992 the *demand* for graduates will have already exceeded supply by 3000 per year. Other commentators describe an equally bleak scenario for other employers. Graduate unemployment is forecast to decrease substantially; graduates themselves are going into an ever widening variety of jobs; and more graduates than ever are becoming self-employed or setting up businesses immediately after graduating.

The problems do not stop with graduates. They extend to school leavers as well. In a forthcoming book on the subject Peter Herriot reports that the number of school leavers in 1992 will be only two-thirds of what it was in the 1980s and goes on to quote a rather chilling example of the consequences for employers. If we continue, he says, 'to expect nurses to start training under 20, to be female, and to have the equivalent of five 'O' levels, we will need more than half of the output of academically able female school leavers'. If this is the NHS demand, then where does that leave banks, building societies, insurance companies or indeed anyone else who employs young people?

To be fair, many companies are already taking steps to counteract these problems (a lot of which are outside the scope of this book, e.g. employing older or even retired people for some jobs), but there are some things employers can do to attract candidates – particularly through the interview.

The first is to recognise that employees *may need to be attracted*. This calls for a fundamental shift in attitudes and norms from some organisations. Employers will need to recognise that the interview is not just about getting information *from* candidates; it can also be used to help give information *to* candidates about the job for which they are applying.

Many psychologists are now beginning to talk in terms of *realistic job previews* and job knowledge questionnaires designed to help candidates make up their minds about whether or not to join an organisation. Interviews can be used to discuss information received by candidates from these previews and employers can use the opportunity of the interview to discuss any problems or worries a candidate may have about taking the job. They can also be used to discuss the terms and conditions on which a person will join an organisation. If, for example, a candidate knows from the realistic job preview that they will need to travel a great deal – but because of domestic circumstances are not able to commit themselves to this – the interview may be used to negotiate a degree of travel that may be acceptable to both the candidate and the organisation.

Of course, organisations will not consider such things lightly. However, in the 1990s they may have to. If they do, the emphasis of the interview may change from one of selection to one of negotiation. In these circumstances an interviewer will need a host of additional skills. Power may shift from the organisation to the candidate, and in this case the organisation may have to use the relatively free flowing interaction between interviewer and candidate to *seduce* the candidate rather than *select* him or her. Information that will enable an organisation to decide whether or not it wants a particular individual may have to be gained at other points in the selection process e.g. testing; assessment centres; or even through structured interviews. The unstructured interview that psychologists have criticised for many years may find a place in the recruitment and selection process of the 1990s – but it is unlikely to be in selecting candidates! It is more likely to be used to *negotiate* with candidates the organisation has already decided that it wants. The interview of the 1990s may be a very different process from the one we have all come to know and expect. Just when we know that some types of interviews can predict job performance, we might want to use it for other things!

A short reading-course on interviews

First, it is best to read chapters giving an overview of research on interviewing e.g.

Landy, F. J. (1985) *Psychology of Work Behaviour*, Chapter 5, Homewood, Illinois, Dorsey Press.

Second, read a key article on situational interviews i.e.

Latham, G. P. *et al.* (1980) 'The situational Interview', *Journal of Applied Psychology*, 65, 422–47.

Third, read a recent meta-analysis of interviews, e.g.

Weisner, W. H. and Cronshaw, S. F. (1988) 'A meta-analytic investigation of the impact of interview format and degree of structure on the validity of the employment interview', *Journal of Occupational Psychology*, 61, **4**, 275–90.

5 Newer methods in selection and assessment: biodata, assessment centres and development centres

The interview remains the most widely used selection instrument at the present time, and in whatever form will continue to be an important part of a manager's toolbox for the foreseeable future. There are, however, other techniques available, all of which have slightly different roles to play in the selection and assessment process. Some have been traditionally used to sift large numbers of applicants, while others are used to make a final decision among a short list of candidates. Some are used primarily when recruiting from outside an organisation; others are used more for internal promotion and career development. In this chapter we will look at two of these assessment techniques – biodata and assessment centres.

Biodata

When faced with, say, 150 application forms for your graduate management trainee scheme, how do you decide who to reject and who to invite for interview? When you read through the forms they all look similar. All the applicants have completed a university course and come out with reasonable degrees; they all say they are ambitious; there isn't any previous work history to judge; they all do their fair share of social activities and look as if they can 'get on with others'. Indeed, why shouldn't the application forms look similar? After all, graduates have tutors and career advisers who will guide them on job applications, how to fill in forms so that they impress people, how to present themselves at interview, etc. In these circumstances the job of sifting application forms is, not surprisingly, very difficult.

So, how do we overcome the problem? Sadly, and often because nothing better exists, we fall back on our own idiosyncrasies. One application has been filled out in black, not blue as requested, therefore it can be rejected without being read at all; another is printed (not written) – or vice versa; another candidate took a year off between school and university and seemed to spend it on an extended holiday; another changed schools three times and so on.

Convenient as these may be as reasons for rejecting applications the problem is that none of these things are *known to relate to job performance*. Sifting application forms on the basis of these idiosyncrasies is like the unstructured interview, a totally subjective process. And, like unstructured interviews, the evidence suggests that as many good candidates slip through the net and are rejected by this method of sifting as get through to the next stage in the selection process. There is, however, an alternative – that of objectively scored biographical data, or 'biodata'.

What are biodata?

Biodata methods are based on the assumption that *either* our characteristics are formed by the experiences we are subjected to in the course of our lives *or* our abilities cause us to select or become involved in certain types of life event. In either case, it follows that if we can accurately assess the events of a person's life, we can deduce something about their skills and abilities.

Owens (1976) defines biodata as a system which allows 'the respondent to describe himself in terms of demographic, experiential, or attitudinal variables presumed or demonstrated to be related to personality structure, personal adjustment or success in social, educational or occupational pursuits'. Biodata are collected on a form which uses a multiple choice format. Many of the items are 'hard' items which seek to provide detailed life history information. For example:

How many brothers or sisters do you have?

None
One
Two
Three
Four or more

These 'hard' items are so called in that they are verifiable. The information could be got from other sources if the organisation so wished. Indeed, on very few occasions the information is obtained from other sources and is terms 'positive vetting'.

Other questions are 'soft' items and cover attitudinal issues or value judgements. For example:

Which of the following has most often caused you to settle for less than you had hoped for?

Your upbringing
Other people
Bad luck
Your qualifications
Something else

These 'soft' items are less easily verifiable and often cause consternation among some occupational psychologists, who describe them as nothing more than ill-defined personality tests. However, they can be of use because although they are open to distortion by candidates they can tap into things which so called 'hard' items cannot – e.g. assertiveness (Drakeley, 1989).

Biodata forms usually contain many questions – some hard and some soft – and differ from application forms in one fundamental respect. With biodata the candidate's answers are combined to produce a score in much the same way as a score is produced if the same candidate completed an ability test. this score is used as the basis for making decisions about the candidate – not the value judgements of the person reading the questionnaire. Cut-off points are set which allow people above the cut-off through to the next stage in the procedure while those who score below the cut-off are rejected.

A typical biodata project

A typical biodata project can be described using an example of a building society recruiting tellers. The number of applications is so large that some efficient first sift is needed to eliminate those candidates with little chance of success so that the available resources can be devoted to giving the fairest possible deal to the remaining candidates. The construction of a biodata system typically proceeds in six stages.

First, a job analysis would be conducted to establish the skills and characteristics needed to perform the job. In our example some of the skills might be: a pleasant approach to people, an eye for detail, persistence and conscientiousness, etc.

Second, a pool of items which seem relevant to these dimensions is created. For example, candidates may be asked to list their leisure activities and the dates during which they have actively pursued them. A tentative scoring method would be devised in which a candidate scores marks for nominating activities involving detailed working or activities which have been pursued for several years (persistence?). The items might be generated in a 'brain storming' session and the scores are, at this stage, tentative.

Third, the questionnaire is given to a large sample of people (e.g. existing employees) for whom criteria, such as supervisory ratings, is available. Generally, the sample should not be smaller than 300 and in any event the size of the sample should be *at least* four times the number of items in the questionnaire.

Fourth, the replies of the sample are subject to statistical analysis to see which combination of questions best predicts successful job performance. At this stage it is also worth doing statistical checks to ensure that no items unfairly disadvantage women or minority groups (a preliminary contextual check for fairness should also be incorporated in stage two).

Fifth, the refined questionnaire is given to applicants, their replies are scored and selection decisions made.

Sixth, the weightings attached to the items in a biodata questionnaire can rapidly become out of date. All biodata systems should therefore incorporate regular studies, perhaps every two years, to check the validity of the scoring key and make adjustments as necessary.

How valid are biodata?

Does biodata work? Do the scores that are produced from the forms correlate with measures of job performance?

Many reviews of biodata have been undertaken, and almost without exception have reported that biodata are among the best predictors of job performance that we have. In their review of different selection techniques, Reilly and Chao (1982) concluded that 'of the alternatives reviewed, only biodata and peer evaluation have evidence of validity equal to that of tests'. The validity of biodata as predictors of job performance is supported by Hunter and Hunter (1984) who, in a meta-analytic study, reported that the three best predictors of entry level performance were ability tests, job try-outs and biodata.

It seems then that biodata work. They predict job performance well, and are therefore a useful part of an organisation's selection systems.

Other reasons for using biodata

Apart from predictive validity biodata have other advantages. Firstly, they are *fair*. The same questions are asked of everyone who completes the form and the answers are scored in exactly the same way. In addition, responses can be *monitored* and individual questions which discriminate against certain groups can be eliminated. Indeed, research has shown that biodata, as a whole, does not have adverse impact on racial groups.

Another reason for using biodata is that they can be very

cost effective. Scoring can be done by anyone and is reduced to a clerical activity. All that needs to be done is to calculate a total score in much the same way as scores are computed in any test. Methods vary, but many of the biodata used by UK companies are scored by entering data directly onto a personal computer. In some cases, the forms are machine read, and at the ultimate level of sophistication, the computer is programmed to write rejection letters to those who score under the cut-off point!

When to use biodata

Biodata are traditionally used for sifting large numbers of applicants applying for a single job or entry level position (e.g. management trainee). It is a pre-selection tool with which companies decide who will be asked to proceed to the next stage of the selection process. As such it is most often used at the graduate or school-leaver level, when decisions have to be made about large numbers of people applying for relatively homogeneous jobs in a short space of time, e.g. apprentice mechanical or electrical engineering.

New horizons in biodata

Biodata have traditionally been used to screen large numbers of applicants for specific jobs or job types. This presupposes that large numbers of people apply for jobs – a situation which may not be such a dominant feature in the 1990s as it was in the 1980s (see Chapter 4 for a brief discussion of how the labour market will change in the next decade). The question therefore needs to be asked, are biodata redundant in a seller's market?

The answer will depend on what organisations want to use biodata for. If they continue to see them in terms of screening large numbers of applicants then the cost effectiveness and applicability of biodata must be questioned. However, organisations need not necessarily see biodata in these terms. It must be remembered that in order to construct a reliable and valid biodata form large numbers of individuals must *already be employed* in the 'target' job. If this is the case, and a reliable and valid biodata form is constructed, the results can predict how well an *individual applicant* is likely to perform in the job. If used in this way biodata still remain a viable assessment tool. In addition they can be used for making *placement* decisions rather than *selection* decisions. For example, if an organisation is selecting into both a sales function and a clerical function, then individual applicants can be assessed for their suitability for either function on the basis of a single application form. Biodata can help allocate people to jobs which suit them most.

It must be recognised, however, that the costs associated with constructing biodata can be prohibitive if an organisation is expecting only a small number of applicants. Therefore some have used an alternative form of personal history information such as 'decision aids'. These are like biodata in that applicants receive a score based on information given on an application form. But they are unlike most biodata in that, whereas traditional biodata uses multiple choice questions to provide a total score, scores on the decision aid are allocated by managers on the basis of narrative information given on a 'normal' application form. In this way 'decision aids' are similar to credit rating forms used in the banking world, and as such can be used with small numbers of applicants.

Finally it must be remembered that one of the things that biodata predict extremely well is turnover. In the seller's market of the 1990s any system that can help identify applicants who are likely to leave an organisation within a short time must be seriously considered. Even though biodata are costly to design, their reliability and validity can quickly provide the utility gains to make the investment worthwhile.

Assessment centres/career development workshops

Assessment centres are not places; they are a process or a procedure. The main characteristic which differentiates assessment centres from other procedures is that they use multiple assessment techniques and multiple assessors to evaluate the skills or personal characteristics of people who attend the centres. These skills and characteristics are observed by the assessors using a structured procedure for making observations and evaluating judgements.

A history of assessment centres

Assessment centres probably owe their origins to the efforts made by the Germans to select military officers in the 1930s. From the beginning of the German military build-up after World War I psychologists were heavily involved with devising procedures to accurately select German officers. Some procedures worked; others didn't – but by the late 1930s a model had emerged which attempted to use the multiple technique, multiple assessor approach.

Although they suffered from many limitations these centres were adapted by the British War Office Selection Boards (WOSBs) in an attempt to quickly and accurately select officers who could help with the war effort. These boards assessed potential officers on a three or four-day programme which involved psychological and psychiatric testing, interviews, and a series of group exercises. The rationale for the exercises is easy to follow. If an officer is expected to lead men in a group, usually under stressful conditions, then what better way to assess his ability to do this than to simulate the conditions in which he will have to operate, and observe his behaviour?

Originally these exercises concentrated on 'planks, ropes and oildrums' but by the end of World War II a greater degree of sophistication had crept in. More emphasis was placed on leaderless group discussions in which problems were set and could be solved only if group members cooperated with each other. In addition, individual exercises were devised, which, together with psychological tests and interviews, helped assessors to evaluate leadership qualities.

These assessment methods spread throughout the military world and were used by other countries including the USA, Australia and Canada. By the 1950s they had developed into sophisticated procedures used with great success in many countries, each with different needs and each with different cultures.

Among the first users of assessment centre techniques

outside a military setting was the British Civil Service. Work on improving the way in which middle and high level civil servants were selected began in 1945. The method used was a three stage process, the second of which was the Civil Service Selection Board (CSSB). This was made up of a number of tests, exercises, interviews, reports and other information, all of which was evaluated by two senior civil service administrators and a psychologist. Successful candidates went on to the Final Selection Board (FSB).

The contribution of CSSB to assessment centres was significant for two reasons. *First* because of the large numbers of candidates to be evaluated, the concept of a multi-stage process was introduced. *Second*, CSSB was the first to apply the techniques of assessment centres to measure administrative and managerial issues, rather than military style leadership.

While CSSB moved assessment centres out of the military sphere, the first *industrial* application was carried out by the American Telegraph and Telephone Company (AT&T). Conceived in the mid 1950s as a management progress study the application was, without doubt, a watershed in the history of assessment centres. AT&T did what many researchers would give their right arms for. They put a large group of junior managers through an assessment centre and then locked up the results for several years. No promotion decisions were made on the basis of assessment centre performance and no feedback was given to line managers about the strengths or weaknesses of the participants. Instead, the results were kept, for a time outside AT&T itself, in order to test whether assessment centre performance predicted future career performance. By doing this AT&T provided the world with an important set of longitudinal data – in other words, data which enabled us to determine the *predictive validity* of assessment centres.

Validity, reliability and fairness of assessment centres

The work at AT&T provided a richness of data unparalleled in the history of assessment centre design or development. Analysis of these data concluded that performance on the centre correlated with job performance. Indeed, rating on the assessment centre predicted the progress of individuals in the organisation through middle and senior management grades.

The validity of assessment centres as predictors of future job performance was therefore established and countless research projects and papers have confirmed that they are certainly among the best we have. Reports from research on CSSB, WOSB, the Admiralty Interview Board and industry itself conclude that assessment centres work. They are expensive to design and run but nevertheless yield a wealth of both qualitative and quantitative data – all of which contribute to an accurate picture of future job performance.

The reliability of assessment centres is also impressive. Again, reports from CSSB, WOSB and industry all suggest that ratings are unlikely to vary if candidates attend more than one centre for a particular job, and that different assessors on the same exercises differ little in their conclusions. Assessment centres are therefore reliable procedures.

When it comes to fairness, assessment centres also come out well. Research suggests that properly designed and run centres do not discriminate against women, nor do they seem to have an adverse impact on protected groups. They are, therefore, among the fairest predictors available. This is because potential is predicted by observing behaviour on job-related dimensions, using job-related exercises. Further, behaviour is observed by trained assessors who individually observe only some of a candidate's performance. In this way a candidate's total performance in the centre is judged by a combination of all the assessors' judgements – it is not left to the subjective judgement of one, possibly biased, assessor.

The use of assessment centres in industry

Because assessment centres are valid, reliable and fair, their popularity has increased significantly in British Industry during the last few years. Indeed, a survey conducted by Robertson and Makin (1986) found that 21 per cent of companies used assessment centres or assessment centre exercises to select managers. This compares with under 10 per cent in the early 1970s, although even within the 21 per cent now using them there is a great deal of variance depending on the size of the organisation. Thirty-six per cent of 'major' recruiters (those recruiting over 100 managers per year) used the technique, while only 10 per cent of 'minor' recruiters (recruiting under ten managers per year) used them.

Although this suggests that many more companies could make use of the techniques available, the results are encouraging. The increased use of more reliable, valid and fair techniques can only be applauded.

So, what form do these assessment centres take? A typical assessment centre will proceed in five stages.

First, a job analysis will identify the key skills and abilities needed to do a job. These skills and abilities are usually called dimensions. Typical dimensions are: leadership, stability, motivation, ability to deal with people, analytical ability, oral communication, written communication. For centres which deal with more top level jobs things such as 'business strategy' and 'organisational sensitivity' can be added to the list. Whichever dimensions are used it is best to keep the number of dimensions below seven. A large number of dimensions make the task of assessors too difficult with the result that the focus becomes imprecise and they respond in terms of global or halo effects. In some assessment centres, the focus of the job analysis is to identify a representative sample of job elements which can then be simulated.

Second, the measures or exercises needed to gauge the dimensions are identified. Usually, this involves preparing a grid with the dimensions down the side and the exercises across the top. In this way, it is easy to identify which exercises measure which dimensions. A golden rule is that each dimension must be gauged by at least two exercises. A minor sophistication is to differentiate between exercises which clearly measure a dimension and those exercises which marginally measure a dimension. Often, these decisions of which measures what are very subjective and may depend on the whims of the psychologist devising the centre. Often these decisions are the weakest link of the assessment centre process.

Third, the precise exercises are developed. They generally come from a selection of the following:

- Leaderless group exercises in which candidates discuss a business problem.
- Assigned group exercises in which each candidate plays the role of a certain manager, e.g. sales, production, purchasing, etc.
- One-to-one counselling, negotiation, or customer meetings in which a candidate is asked to run a meeting. The customer, employee or trade union official is played by a role player.
- Presentation type exercises in which candidates are asked to prepare a presentation and then deliver it to an assessor.
- Paper and pencil analytical exercises in which candidates analyse written and numerical information and then write a report on it.
- 'In-tray' exercises in which candidates sort through a typical in-tray and decide on various priorities and actions.

Also, because assessment centres use multiple techniques there is nothing to stop organisations incorporating information from other methods. Structured interviews are often included in the centres, as are ability tests and personality questionnaires – and some centres even include self or peer ratings.

An important part in the production of the exercises is the development of detailed scoring methods. In principle, there should be a behaviourally anchored rating scale for each dimension measured by an exercise.

Fourth, administrative arrangements are made. A fairly typical centre will last two days and will involve six candidates, three assessors and one psychologist. An important administrative aspect is the selection and training of the assessors. It is important that the assessors should be managers one or two levels higher in the organisation than the 'target' job. Assessors are asked to observe specific candidates on specific exercises, and a schedule needs to be drawn up to ensure that at any given time a candidate is independently observed by at least two assessors and that during the course of the centre each candidate will be observed, in roughly equal proportions, by all assessors. *Fifth,* the data from the assessment centres must be evaluated. Traditionally, these are known as 'wash up' sessions and take place the day after the centre. The assessors meet to discuss the information obtained and to derive a score for the candidates. Sometimes, there is a decision to give some exercises or dimensions greater weight than others. For example, the more reliable methods of measurement might be given twice the weighting of less reliable ones, and key characteristics such as stability and intelligence might be given twice the weighting of other dimensions. Recent research has cast some doubt on the necessity for such wash up sessions – it suggests that it is more accurate simply to add up the scores without discussion.

New horizons in assessment centres

There are two new horizons in assessment centres. The first is a technical issue and the second is a practical one.

The technical issue is a debate among practitioners and psychologists about whether assessment centres should try to measure performance by *dimension* (as is traditional) or by *exercise.* This debate is based on evidence both from the States and from Britain that assessors do not differentiate a candidate's performance by dimension, but by exercise. In other words, if a candidate was being measured on, say, interpersonal skills, decision making, planning and organising and flexibility, it is likely that, over the centre as a whole, the average rating on each of these would be very similar. On the other hand, if these very same dimensions were being measured by, say, an in-tray, a group exercise, a one-to-one negotiation exercise and a presentation exercise, it is likely that the candidate would be given significantly different marks for the various exercises.

This finding has many implications for assessment centres,

not least for how they are designed. To begin with, it implies that exercises *must* be job-related. Employers really do not need to know who builds the best tower out of string and sellotape! Secondly, it puts a great deal of emphasis on a thorough job analysis. If exercises do discriminate better than dimensions it is important to sample fully the job in the centre. There is no point in covering only half the job in the centre, even if all the necessary traits or dimensions are adequately sampled.

The second new horizon in assessment centres is the increasing use of them to identify potential *within* an organisation as opposed to selecting candidates from outside. Based on the same principles as selection centres (i.e. multiple assessors, multiple techniques) these 'development' centres have a very different philosophy. One of the best expositions of the differences between assessment centres and development centres was given by Scott Kerr and Hugh Davenport (1989) based on their experiences within British Telecom. Some of the key differences are:

- Development centres are usually longer and measure more dimensions.
- A climate must be created in which it is 'ok' to make mistakes.
- Review time is included in the programme and assessees are given feedback during the programme itself. The feedback should focus on positive suggestions and the amount is limited in order not to overwhelm assessees. There is then a second chance to practise the positive points.
- Observers do not remain 'detached' and critical. The participants share in the process and help understanding by adopting the roles of co-learners and facilitators.
- Exercises of moderate rather than high difficulty are used.
- The centre should be preceded by a questionnaire before work on self, peer and superior assessment.
- There is a natural progression of emphasis from care skill building, to observed exercises, to feedback, and the centre ends with a large component of counselling and action planning.

Apart from the reliability and validity of the approach the most far reaching implication about these centres is something which is not immediately obvious. The centres are not confined to middle or junior management – indeed there are often too many job incumbents at these levels to consider using these techniques for everyone. Rather they are being used to identify potential directors and senior managers. The observers are therefore existing directors and senior managers (including chief executives on some occasions). The involvement of these people in such detailed assessment and development impacts on the organisation in a way which far exceeds the initial objective of identifying and nurturing potential. It creates a commitment to objective assessment and development that is usually unparalleled in the organisation's history.

A short reading course

First, consult a general text on assessment centres such as Moses and Byham, W.C. (1977) *Applying the Assessment Centre Method,* New york, Pergamon.
Second, consult descriptions and evaluations of specific assessment centres. For example, Anstey, E. (1977) 'A thirty year follow up of the CSSB procedure with lessons for the future', *Journal of Occupational Psychology,* 50, 149–59.
Third, read some of the articles dealing with the issue of dimensions vs exercises e.g. Robertson, I.T., Gratton, L. and Sharpley, D. (1987) 'The psychometric properties of managerial assessment centres: Dimensions into exercises won't go', *Journal of Occupational Psychology,* 60, **3**, 187–96.
Finally, read an account of the differences between assessment centres and development centres, e.g. Kerr, S. and Davenport, H. (1989) 'AC or DC? The Experience of Development Centres. Proceedings of BPS Symposium', *British Telecom Occupational Psychologists: Developing the Developers,* British Telecom Management and Commercial College, Derby House, 219 Queensway, Bletchley, MK2 2DQ.

Further reading on biodata

There is much less readily available published data on biodata. A good starting place is: Owens, W.A. (1976) 'Background Data' in Dunnette, M.D. (ed.) *Handbook of Industrial and Organisational Psychology,* Chicago, Rand McNally.

A recent example of the use of biodata is:

Drakeley, R.J. (1989) 'Biographical Data' in Herriot, P.l (ed) *The Handbook of Assessment in Organisations,* Chichester, Wiley (in press).

6 Recent advances in psychometric testing

During the last decade the use of tests has increased quite dramatically, but tests remain a relatively rare method of selection. A fairly subjective estimate would be that about five per cent of applicants are given some type of test. For graduates and management the probability will certainly be higher than average. Testing is also higher in sales jobs and jobs involved in the transport industry, e.g. pilots, air traffic controllers or train drivers. The low level of test use represents a paradox since tests are some of the most accurate methods of selection, and meta-analyses routinely return validities in the region of 0.5. This can be contrasted with typical interviews which, arguably, are used in 95 per cent of selections but which routinely return validities of below 0.2. A cynic might observe that industry's preference for selection methods is in inverse proportion to their accuracy.

Types of test: analytical or analogous

Broadly speaking there are two types of test: analytical tests and analogous tests. Sometimes the two types are referred to as psychological tests and work sample tests, and sometimes they are called signs and samples.

In a nutshell, *analytical tests* analyse job performance into fundamental human characteristics, such as intelligence, sociability or manual dexterity. They then measure these abilities by evoking behaviour which may not have any apparent similarity with the behaviour on the job. Predictions of actual job performance are made by weighting an applicant's scores according to a formula. *Analogous tests*, on the other hand, attempt to replicate the key activities involved in the job. There is a point-to-point correspondence between the tasks involved in the test and the tasks involved in the job. Predictions of job performance are direct. Both types of test may be viewed as good predictors but the evidence suggests that analogous tests have the edge on analytical tests, say, respective validities of 0.54 and 0.53. But, the margin is so small that other factors need to be taken into account.

Analogous tests (work samples)

Analogous tests are based upon the analysis of specific tasks. The test constructor tries to produce a miniature version of a task which contains most of the key elements of the job. In this way a point-to-point correspondence is achieved. It is this point-to-point correspondence which gives analogous tests their main advantages: a slightly better predictive power, and greater acceptability to the organisation and applicant. Analogous or work sample tests capture some of the contextual factors as well as the basic human abilities. For example, a building society may produce a work sample for branch managers which requires him or her to prepare weekly accounts for the branch. Inevitably, this work sample will measure the basic abilities of numerical reasoning and, say, communication skills. But the work sample will also include contextual factors such as the size of numbers and reporting conventions adopted by that particular society.

Mastery of the contextual factors may well be a significant aspect of mastery of the job – at least in the shorter term. The contextual factors may also have an important psychological impact on the applicant. They may give an impression of realism resulting in higher motivation and a view that the testing procedure is fair and reasonable. There may be yet another advantage. Two or three work samples give the applicant a very clear picture of what the job involves. There is some evidence that if people have a clear view of the job they are more likely to start their employment and they are less likely to leave the job in the first few weeks.

Most of the advantages of analogous tests stem from the

specificity of the work sample, but so do the disadvantages. A good work sample will be based on a specific job or a specific group of jobs. Many of the contextual details will be inappropriate for other jobs. Work samples are less 'transportable' than analytical tests. They usually apply to relatively large-scale selection situations. Because they may be relevant to only small numbers of candidates few resources are available for development. Often, the standardisation of work samples is poor and the reliability and validity are unknown. For example, an organisation will allocate about a week of a psychologist's time to develop an in-basket for its selection programme for six management trainees. The resources devoted to the development of an intelligence test which can be obtained 'off the shelf' will be months if not years.

A final problem with work samples is that they may disadvantage those who are quite good at the basic requirements of a task but who, for some reason, are unfamiliar with the precise context. It may be claimed that they are not good at identifying talent. Someone who has had years of experience in a specific situation will obtain a high score. Someone who has higher ultimate potential but no experience in the context of the work sample will fare less well.

The content of the work sample does, and must, vary greatly with the job involved. Probably the most ubiquitous work sample is the typing test. It is probably ninety per cent certain that anyone applying for a typing job will be sat in front of a typewriter and asked to type a piece of work. In most cases the instructions, the task and the scoring will be so haphazard and sloppy that the method will hardly qualify as a test. Work samples are easy to construct for manual jobs, for exmple, in a work sample for a skilled craft such as bricklaying, an applicant would be asked to lay a course of bricks, which incorporates several important and representative aspects of the craft.

Work samples are also particularly easy to construct in jobs involving social contact such as salespeople, bank tellers or librarians. For example, an applicant could be asked to role play the part of a salesman who visits a customer only to find the customer preoccupied with a complaint about a defect. Many work samples for management fall into this category. Management may also involve other work samples such as:

- in-tray (in-basket) tests;
- group problem solving in which the group must come to a conclusion which is satisfactory to all (e.g. the sequence in which departments should be moved to a new headquarters building);
- group problem solving in which there will be winners and losers – e.g. a simulated budget allocation meeting;
- a presentation in which the candidate can choose the topic;
- a presentation in which the topic is chosen for the candidate;
- a counselling role play in which the applicant is asked to counsel a 'subordinate' whose performance is unsatisfactory;
- report writing and problem solving on the basis of a file which contains realistic and relevant facts.

An interesting variation on work sample tests is the 'trainability tests' developed by Sylvia Downs. As the name implies, the object of these tests is to predict a person's suitability for training. Often training can be very expensive and the employment of people who quit or fail training is a waste of resources. Trainability tests aim to set up 'point-to-point correspondence' between a test and training situation. Perhaps the classic example is a trainability test for sewing machinists. Applicants are first asked to sew around three sides of a piece of fabric to make a bag. Their efforts are scored according to a carefully worked out scheme. The applicants are then given a short period of instruction about how to use the machine, turn corners and finish the piece of work, etc. Finally, applicants are asked to make a second bag and their efforts are again scored. The main point is not their actual scores but the *improvement* between the scores on the first and the second bags.

Analytical tests

There is no clear line dividing analytical and analogous tests. Indeed, some writers have suggested a continuum, with analogous tests measuring specific and crystallised abilities at one end and analytical tests measuring general, fluid abilities at the other. Somewhere in the middle are pencil and paper trade tests such as tests of computer programming ability or some pencil and paper tests of inspection tasks.

Most analytical tests can be subdivided into three groups according to the type of human ability they purport to measure: ability tests, personality tests and tests of motivation.

Tests of ability

Tests of ability cover physical ability and mental ability. The physical ability tests may include measures of such things as manual dexterity or coordination. They may also include some sensory tests such as colour blindness or hearing.

Psychologists tend to focus upon mental ability. The most usual measure is general mental ability which is something akin to 'intelligence'. The next most important measures under this category are measures of verbal reasoning and numerical reasoning. Sometimes, measures of spatial, mechanical or other specific abilities are used. Good tests of mental ability had been developed by 1970. But recently test publishers have developed a range of new ones. There is no evidence to suggest that new tests are any better, or any worse, than existing tests. Their development arose from commercial not scientific needs. However, modern tests usually have better graphical design and their visual appeal may help gain the cooperation and support of others.

A significant development in the last decade has been the production of 'trade tests' for modern occupations. For example, there have been new tests for computer programmers, systems analysts, people working on word processors and people working in automated offices.

Many publishers have also brought out computer versions of tests. Usually, there have been simple modifications of existing ones. The advantages of computer versions of existing tests may be quite dubious. Indeed, they may cost more than traditional pencil and paper methods. As a later section of this chapter shows, simple minded adaptations miss some of the huge potential of computer testing.

Personality tests

Early attempts to measure personality bordered on the insane. For example, the Rorschach test required candidates to gaze into inkblots. We now know that such techniques are rarely valid and it is doubtful whether the inkblot test has been used in any serious way for over 20 years.

Some of the early personality questionnaires used in selection were questionnaires from clinical settings. One of the most popular was the Minnesota Multiphasic Personality Inventory. The MMPI was originally developed to differentiate between psychotics, psychopaths and neurotics, etc. It was of some use in industry. But, out of context, some of the questions looked quite strange. For example, senior executives would be asked questions such as 'do you check the colour of your water as you urinate?' Actually this is not a bad question for detecting hypochondriacs but it is a bizarre question to ask a chief executive of a multinational company! The use of clinical based questionnaires has declined and now they are used very rarely indeed.

Other personality tests are based on a priori theories. Usually they are some derivative of psychoanalytical theories. One example is the Myers Briggs Type Indicator. The test is based on Jung's theories of the early 1920s. It typecasts people into a system of 16 categories:

- introverts or extroverts
- objective or intuitive
- logical or emotional
- decisive and purposeful or hesitant and reflective

Tests such as the Myers-Briggs can be criticised on grounds other than their psychoanalytical roots. First, many such tests are ipsative. As noted later, ipsative tests should not be used in selection. Second, many selectors cavil at placing people into discreet types. It is known that people's personalities are arranged along a continuum and not in watertight compartments.

Modern tests of personality are empirically derived. A large sample of people are asked a wide range of questions. Their replies are scrutinised to see if there are any consistent themes. This scrutiny is usually a statistical procedure called factor analysis. Sometimes, the scrutiny is by a panel of experts or consultants. The results from empirical analyses have been surprisingly consistent. But, this consistency has been masked by the need to use different terms in order to keep the laws of copyright. There are also commercial needs to give tests a distinctive appearance in the market-place. Another cause of confusion is the level of analysis. Extroversion has been repeatedly identified as a major factor. Some tests subdivide this factor into its component parts, such as being outgoing, social confidence and affiliation. So, it appears that two tests are measuring different things. In fact, it is merely a matter of one of the tests looking at the same thing in greater detail.

Four major trends in personality have been identified:

- extroversion – introversion
- stability – neuroticism
- tough-mindedness – tender-mindedness
- independence – dependence

There is some suggestion that these factors may have a neurological basis. For example, there is the idea that the neural systems of introverts transmit messages very readily. Thus, they receive the full blast of the stimulation of their environment. To counteract this, introverts tend to be quiet people who seek 'quiet environments'. There is another idea that stability is related to a person's automatic nervous system. This is the branch of the nervous system controlling reactions such as sweating or heart pounding which our minds interpret as emotion. Finally, there is some suggestion that toughness is related to the level of arousal in the cortex of the brain. The cortex is the brain area responsible for conscious thought.

There have been three major empirical tests of personality: the Eysenck Personality Inventory, The Guilford-Zimmerman Temperament Survey and the 16PF scales. The EPI is probably the least used in selection. It is a simple questionnaire and many candidates resent having to give either a yes or a no answer to questions. In addition the EPI has some questions which seem to be slanted to clinical settings. The Guilford-Zimmerman is an excellent questionnaire but there has been no recent standardisation. Comparisons can only be made with the population as it was some time ago. Some consultants have maintained their own set of norms and continue to obtain good results. But the lack of up-to-date norms means that the use of the Guilford-Zimmerman has declined and now it is rarely used.

These factors have left the field clear for the 16PF to become the pre-eminent test of personality in selection. In fact there are four versions of this test: A, B, C and D. There are also objective scales (the O – A Tests) but these are cumbersome and rarely used. Versions C and D were developed for special purposes *and should not be used in selection*. Because of its pre-eminence, the 16PF has been very widely researched and a great deal of data has been amassed. Equations exist to calculate leadership potential, ability to grow into a new job and the type of team role a person will adopt. In addition, 16PF profiles exist for almost 100 occupations.

During the last five years the hegemony of the 16PF has been challenged by the Occupational Personality Questionnaire (Saville Holdsworth). This is perhaps the only personality test designed specifically for use in industrial settings. In fact it is not a single questionnaire but a series of interlocking questionnaires. The selector chooses the test which gives the necessary level of detail. It is too early to give a definitive evaluation of the OPQ but the signs are looking very good.

The possibilities of deception are a continuous concern. Counter measures are often taken. Test constructors try to produce tests that are resistant to deception by asking questions where the 'correct' response is not apparent. Test constructors may also try to detect and measure the extent to which a person is lying. The EPI, the 16PF and the OPQ all have scales to measure social desirability or lying. Because of these efforts lying may not work. In one experiment a group of people were taught how to lie on personality tests using the rules set out in Whyte's book *The Organisation Man*. Another group was given no such coaching. Profiles from both groups were given to practising personnel managers who rated individuals on their suitability. Those who had attempted to lie received poorer ratings.

Many tests of personality are of dubious accuracy. The following rules of thumb are offered to help screen out the less acceptable ones.

- Ask an organisation to send you, by post, copies of the questionnaires and answer keys. Be careful not to reveal any qualifications or experience you have in psychology, testing or personnel management. If the tests are sent to you without knowledge of these facts beware of the test. Tests are usually sold on a confidential basis to those who are qualified not to misuse them.
- Ask if it is permissible to send the candidates the tests to complete by mail. If the answer is yes, beware of the test. If it is sent through the post conditions of administration cannot be controlled and in some cases the person who has answered may not be the candidate.
- Ask how many questions the test contains and ask how many separate 'things' the test measures (i.e. scales). Divide the questions by the scales and if there are fewer than about 10 questions per scale beware of the test. It is well known that in most situations the accuracy of a test is related to its length. If there are fewer than 10 questions per scale it is highly likely that the chance factors associated with individual questions do not have the opportunity to cancel each other out.
- Look at the type of questions to see if they are ipsative. Ipsative questions are those where the candidate is forced to make a choice between several alternatives. Each alternative is relevant to a different scale. For example, one question on the Myers Briggs test might be:

Do you think it is worse to be
(*a*) an action oriented person
(*b*) someone who is sensitive to the feelings of others?

The problem with this type of question is that it is possible to be *both* action oriented and sensitive. The results from a series of questions of this kind can be quite misleading. They can show the *pattern* of someone's personality: i.e. they can show that you are more action oriented than sensitive. Even so you can still be much more sensitive than most other people.

An important question is 'how accurate are personality tests?' At first sight the answer to this question is discouraging. Meta-analyses indicate that the average validity of a single scale on a personality test is about 0.16. This is almost certainly a misleading figure. It is the average of all scales for all jobs. But some aspects of personality are irrelevant in some jobs. The real question is 'what is the validity of the combination of relevant scales?' Meta-analyses to answer this question are only just starting. A tentative answer would be about 0.45.

Latent trait theory and item response theory

The honest observer will admit that there have been few developments in the basis of psychological testing. But there have been major cosmetic changes in design and huge improvements in marketing. On the horizon are some important theoretical developments. These could transform the way that we test people. The theory which has governed testing for half a century has been the true score plus error model. According to this model each question has a level of difficulty. In individual cases, this level of difficulty is surrounded by a margin of error. The margin of error reflects chance factors such as experience and the way the applicant feels on the day they are tested. The way to minimise the error is to ask lots of questions so that the chance factors can cancel out. A test will therefore include questions at all levels of difficulty and everyone will attempt all questions. The final score will be the number of correct answers.

The true score plus error approach has been strongly criticised. In academic and theoretical circles it is being replaced by item response theory. In due course, these developments will have an impact on the way in which organisations test applicants. In the past the emphasis has lain on the scores from scales. Item response theory lays emphasis on the individual question.

IRT says that there are basic traits. Questions can be positioned on these traits according to 'their level of difficulty'. By knowing the questions a candidate 'just' gets right, their level of ability can be calculated. Usually, the calculations require two pieces of information about each question: the level of difficulty, and the degree to which the question can discriminate between able people and stupid people.

In traditional tests the estimate of ability is based on the replies to a standard set of questions. IRT produces estimates of ability based on different sets of questions. For example, in a traditional test of intelligence everyone is given the same 120 or so questions and an estimate of ability is derived from the replies to all the questions. In item response theory a candidate is given only a few questions. Stupid candidates may be given only 15 easy questions. Average candidates will be given 15 or so average questions; bright candidates will be given 15 or so difficult questions. Although candidates may be given different questions, their level of ability on the same scale can be gauged because the difficulty of the questions is known.

The basics of item response theory have been known for decades. The new horizons arise because computers can utilise these theories to make testing more efficient. The computer can give one question and on the basis of the answer it can calculate the level of ability on the latent trait. The computer can then check out its deductions by administering other questions at the level of difficulty indicated by its calculations. In this way testing becomes much more efficient. Candidates are not presented with reams of questions that are too easy. Similarly, questions that are much too difficult are also avoided. There is evidence that 13 questions carefully selected according to IRT are more accurate than a traditional test of, say, 130 questions.

Item response theory is quite unwieldy. A computer is needed to calculate which questions are most relevant for each candidate. But ITR does no more than scratch the surface of the potential in using computers in psychometric testing. Computers can present entirely different types of questions from those presented on the printed page. Potential questions can use movement, colour, sound, enhancement and facing. Just over the horizon is a new genre of computer administered tests which will bear little relation to today's rather pathetic adaptation of the tests which were developed in the middle years of this century.

Further reading

Holland, P. W. and Rubin, D. B. (1982) *Test Equating*, Orlando, FL, Academic Press.

Johnson, C. E., Wood, R. and Blinkhorn, S. F. (1988) 'Spuriouser and spuriouser: the use of ipsative personality tests', *Journal of Occupational Psychology*, 61, **2**, 153–62.

Lumsden, J. (1976) 'Test Theory', *Annual Review of Psychology*, 27, 154–80.

Toplis, J., Dulewicz, V. and Fletcher, C. (1987), *Psychological Testing: a practical guide*. London, Institute of Personnel Managers.

Rasch, G. (1966) 'An individualistic approach to item analysis', in Lazarsfeld, P. F. and Henry, N. W. (eds) *Readings in Mathematical Social Sciences*, 89–107, Cambridge, MA, MIT Press.

Addresses of test publishers

Assessment and Selection for Employment (NFER/Nelson), Darville House, 2 Oxford Road East, Windsor, Berkshire, SL4 1DF (Tel. 0753-858961; telex 24966001; fax 0753 856830).

The Psychological Corporation, Foots Cray High Street, Sidcup, Kent, DA14 5HP (Tel. 01-300-1149).

Saville Holdsworth Ltd., The Old Post House, 81 High Street, Esher, Surrey, KT10 9QA (Tel. 0372-68634; telex 935505; fax 0372 62374).

Science Research Associates, Newton Road, Henley-on-Thames, Oxfordshire, RG9 1EW (Tel. 0491-575959; telex 848454).

7 More controversial methods of selection: graphology, astrology, lie detectors, etc.

The ways in which some organisations select their personnel are, to say the least, weird and wonderful. In the splot technique the managers who are contenders for top level positions in their organisation are taken for a weekend to a farm house. On the Friday evening they are given a supply of twelve pellets of red ink and a gun which fires them. Their task is to fire the pellets to hit their rivals while at the same time avoiding being hit themselves. The contenders are left to their own devices to 'enjoy' the weekend. When the selectors return on the Monday morning they simply count the number of splots on the candidates' clothing and the executive with the fewest splots is offered promotion.

Except in quite unusual circumstances, the splot technique is clearly a travesty of good selection. However, the fact that a technique is unusual or unorthodox does not necessarily mean that it is useless. This chapter will examine six of these methods: self assessment, peer assessment, graphology, astrology, honesty testing, accomplishment record and the future autobiography. The central issue with all of these techniques is, do they work?

Finding out if a selection method works

A method of selection can only be said to work if it survives scientific examination which eliminates the possibilities of fraud, coincidence or a more likely alternative explanation. Over the years psychology has established the requirements for scientific studies. Some of the requirements are as follows.

The *sample* on which a conclusion is based plays a large part in determining whether a study is scientifically sound. There are two main requirements: the sample must be unbiased and the sample should be reasonably large. Clearly, a sample that is based only on favourable instances is useless. Anecdotal evidence nearly always falls into this category. Enthusiasts of any method can usually select several cases where their favourite method has worked. For example, if challenged, many astrologers will be able to quote instances where their method has worked. But, either consciously or subconsciously they may have selected only their successes and they may have forgotten a much larger number of failures. The only real test is for them to specify, *in advance*, the sample and then to look at the results for the whole sample.

The sample should also be large – certainly over 30 and preferably over 300. It is a fundamental law of statistics that small samples give erratic results. If very small samples are used, then, by the laws of chance alone, a noticeable proportion of these samples will produce positive results. The proponents of a method will focus upon these studies to show that the method works in the 'right circumstances'. In all studies, the results should be compared to what would happen by chance alone – this process is usually referred to as testing for statistical significance.

In a good study, the person making the predictions will know nothing about the actual performance of the subject concerned. Technically, this is usually referred to as making *'blind' predictions*. For example, an organisation may decide to test out the accuracy of an astrologer by seeing if he or she could differentiate between a group of operatives and a group of sales assistants. Clearly, the astrologer should not know to which group an individual belongs when they are making predictions about that individual because any success might be due to this extra knowledge rather than the merits of astrology. A recent study at UMIST used this method. By the laws of chance the astrologer should get 50 per cent of the nominations correct. In fact his success rate was only 48 per cent. Contamination of the predictions by extra knowledge may be quite subtle. For example, a graphologist could pick up enough information from the quality of paper used or the vocabulary of what is written to give enough clues to raise the level of the predictions above the chance level. The graphologists themselves may not be aware that they are responding to these clues rather than the actual handwriting.

In a good study, the subject and others who influence their performance will have no knowledge of the predictions until after performance has been measured. If this requirement is violated then the results could be attributed to *a self fulfilling prophesy*. For example, a managing director who has great faith in astrology may seek astrological advice on the appointment of functions heads. A year after receiving the astrologer's reports he or she is quite likely to find that there is some correspondence between these reports and the performances of his executive team. This correspondence may well be due to the self fulfilling prophesy rather than the effectiveness of astrology. If the managing director has a strong belief in astrology he or she is likely to take the reports seriously. Those function heads with favourable reports are likely to be given greater encouragement, support or scope – in other words their performance will be enhanced and may well account for better objective performance.

If the managing director uses his or her own opinions as a measure of performance, the situation is even worse because the knowledge of what is contained in the reports could directly influence his or her subsequent judgements. The candidates should also be unaware of the predictions made about them because those with a good prediction may be encouraged and try harder whilst someone with a poor prediction may give up trying.

People also tend to live up to stereotypes and the effects can be quite subtle. For example, there is a statistically significant tendency for people with certain zodiac signs to rate themselves as extroverts. However, roughly half the population know enough about astrology to be aware of the characteristics associated with their sign of the zodiac. One investigation gave subjects a test of knowledge of astrology and eliminated those who knew the characteristics of their star sign. This subsample were then asked to rate themselves on extroversion. It was found that in this group the link between extroversion and birth sign did not exist. The initial effect was caused by some people living up to common stereotypes.

Once these requirements of scientific investigation have been set out it is possible to start answering the question whether the more controversial methods of selection work.

Self assessment

In many ways, getting candidates to assess themselves is an alluring possibility. The procedure is likely to be quick and cheap. Furthermore, the individuals should know a great deal about themselves since only they have observed their reactions to the wide range of situations that have made up their lives. Surely, with such a rich and comprehensive source of information self assessments must be fairly accurate?

Unfortunately there is an equal or greater number of impediments. First, the person may not know the qualities needed for the job concerned. An outsider who has experience of the work may be in a better position to come to a conclusion. Second, the person may not be able to use the data base about him or herself in a very effective way. It may be that some individuals are just lousy at drawing conclusions about people, and there is no reason to suppose that judgements about themselves are any better. An outside person who can compare the behaviours of, say, six candidates may be in a better position to draw conclusions than someone who has only their own behaviour as a standard. Judgements about ourselves may well be systematically biased. There is very good evidence that we overestimate our abilities. In one study, for example, typists were found to over-estimate their typing speed by 30 per cent. Third, even if we can come to an accurate assessment of our own abilities, there remains the question of whether people are prepared to reveal these estimates truthfully in an employment situation.

The only way of settling such arguments is to look at the empirical evidence. Unfortunately this evidence is sparse. In 1982 Reilly and Chao combined the results of three studies which gave a total sample size of 545. The average weighted validity of 0.15 was obtained. In 1988 George and Smith reported another validity study on 176 seasonal workers in New Zealand and obtained validity coefficients of 0.19 with appraised job performance and 0.21 with labour turnover. Weighting these figures with the findings of Reilly and Chao gives a validity coefficient of about 0.16.

Peer ratings

Peer ratings – or buddy ratings as the Americans call them – have been around for quite some time and have almost as much allure as self ratings. There are three main advantages. First, peers or colleagues see a great deal of a candidate's behaviour and they also have first-hand insight into the jobs they do. Second, the ratings are usually based on the views of several people and consequently subjectivities and errors have a chance to cancel each other out. Third, ratings are usually cheap and convenient to collect. Fourth, buddy ratings are demonstrably democratic and are therefore appealing to those organisations who want to be in the van of the 'greater participation' movement.

Unfortunately, peer ratings have their downside arguments too: the buddies may not be adept at making judgements of other people; in highly cohesive groups they may be quite reluctant to give frank assessments in case they cause damage and humiliation to an inter-dependent colleague; or they may manipulate their ratings in a way which they believe will give them a tactical advantage over a potential rival. Perhaps the most biting theoretical criticism of buddy ratings is that buddies usually only have evidence of performance in the present job. This means that they have limited use for either initial hiring or promotion decisions.

Since the arguments for or against peer assessments are closely balanced it is necessary to look at the empirical evidence. Early studies conducted around the 1950s quickly established that peer ratings are very reliable and coefficients of 0.9 were routinely obtained. The more important question of the validity of the method had to wait until the meta-analyses of the 1980s to produce an acceptable estimate. The precise validity of peer assessment depends upon several factors, especially the type of criteria that are used (e.g. promotion or performance), but Reilly and Chao suggest that the average validity of peer assessments is 0.41 (based upon a total sample of 12,749). A meta-analysis by Hunter and Hunter suggests a validity of 0.49.

On this basis the future of buddy ratings is quite bright, especially since the methods of actually collecting the ratings were quite crude. There is, however, one cloud on the horizon. Peer ratings may not be popular with the people involved. One study in 1980 found that 59 per cent of those involved in systems of this kind were in favour of the discontinuation of the system.

Graphology

The acceptance of graphology as a method of personnel selection seems to show wide cultural variation. In the UK and USA it is infrequently used: a student project at UMIST revealed that in 1980 only 2 of 71 companies from the *Times 1,000 Guide* who replied to a survey admitted to using graphology in their organisation. In continental Europe, however, graphology is more widely accepted. At a meeting of 270 delegates to the World Congress of Handwriting in Amsterdam in 1966, 73 delegates came from France, 53 from Germany and a mere eight from the UK.

Many systems have tried to use handwriting to predict personality. The simplest, and most scientific methods have used physical characteristics such as pressure on the page or speed of writing. The second approach focuses upon single features such as slant, regularity and connections between letters. The third, holistic approach is the method adopted by most graphologists and uses complex analyses which are based on combinations of features.

Unfortunately, many of the studies of graphology have been flawed by many of the problems outlined earlier in this chapter. But in 1983 Klimoski and Rafaeli conducted a review of the available evidence. Their main findings were as follows.

- People's handwriting is fairly stable – certainly over a period of several months. However, data not included by Klimoski and Strickland show that handwriting can change according to the will of the writer. Most people can improve the neatness of their writing when they want to create a good impression, such as when they are writing application forms. In one study, students were asked to fake the handwriting of methodical people or of original people. Subsequent judgements by others indicated that the students were largely successful in their attempts at deception.
- Graphologists tend to be consistent in the conclusions they draw from handwriting despite the fact that they may be using rather different techniques. Indeed, graphologists tend to be more consistent than interviewers.
- Graphology could not predict the success of salespeople in terms of annual sales turnover.
- Graphology could not predict whether the people were energetic or passive.
- Graphologists cannot identify people who are diagnosed as neurotic.
- Graphologists were able to distinguish between real and 'spoofed' suicide notes.
- Professional training does not seem to improve the accuracy of a graphologist's predictions.

As a general conclusions Klimoski and Rafaeli comment, 'Although the literature on this topic suffers from significant methodological negligence, the general trend of findings is to suggest that graphology is not a viable assessment method.'

More recent evidence has supported Klimoski and Rafaeili's conclusion. Yet another investigation has come to the conclusion that graphology is no better than chance, but this time the investigators were Israeli. It would seem that graphology does not work in Hebrew either!

Astrology

In some cultures, and apparently even in some high places in Western cultures, the suitability of applicants may be referred to astrologers. Astrology requires some kind of mystical faith because there is no known scientific link between the position of heavenly bodies, light years away, and the ability of someone to do the job.

There is a great deal of anecdotal evidence to support the use of astrology – mainly people pointing to the accuracy of their horoscope. Such successes can often be attributed to the well known 'fortune teller effect': the horoscopes are couched in such general terms that they apply to almost everyone (e.g., in the next month you will meet a stranger, you will go on a journey, etc., etc.). People are more likely to believe in a horoscope if it is favourable.

The evidence on the actual accuracy of horoscopes is very negative. In 1979 a prize of £500 was offered to anyone who could provide valid scientific evidence of the link between sun signs and personality. The prize remains unclaimed. One investigator reviewed the evidence on astrology and made the Churchillian comment, 'never before in history has so much been based on so little by so many'.

A classic example of the genre of research into astrology examined the birth dates of 7,233 artists and musicians. According to most astrological schools of thought, the zodiac sign of Libra is ruled by Venus and has clear associations with the arts. Yet, analysis showed the Librans were no more common as artists or musicians than any other zodiac sign. Other studies have found that there is no relationship between the birth signs of university students and the subjects they study.

However, there remains one set of investigations which seem to stand up to most scientific requirements. These studies involve not the sun signs (i.e. the familiar zodiac signs) but the position of the planets at the time of birth. Two French investigators, Michel and Francoise Gauquelin noticed a slight tendency, in *very* eminent people, for the planets to be in certain positions at the time of birth. For example, there was a slight tendency for 2088 European sportsmen of international standing to be born when Mars was either just over the horizon or had just passed its highest point in the sky. This has subsequently been known as the Mars Effect. Similar effects have been shown for other eminent groups – for example, eminent scientists tend to have Saturn rising or just overhead and for writers it tends to be the moon which is in these positions.

The work of the Gauquelins has caused considerable controversy but it has generally stood up to scrutiny. The findings must, however, be placed in context. They only apply for very eminent people and the effect is too weak to be of any practical significance in terms of employee selection.

Honesty testing

It is not unreasonable for employers to specify honesty as a key requirement for employees. In many organisations, especially in the finance and retail sectors, the honesty of employees is a key concern. It is also a growing concern in the data processing function as the potential for computer fraud increases. There have been two main approaches to selecting honest employees: lie detectors and honesty tests.

Lie detectors

Lie detectors are based on the idea that when people are consciously lying it is natural for them to be anxious. Anxiety is usually accompanied by physical symptoms such as increased sweating, deeper breathing, muscle tension, increased pulse and greater brain activity. These increases are usually hard to detect with the naked eye but they can be detected by electronic devices and output on a roll of continuous paper. The device is usually called a polygraph because it graphs several aspects of anxiety. Generally, a lie detector examination starts with a series of innocuous questions to establish a base rate. Then the examination can proceed in two ways. In the *guilty knowledge technique* a suspect is asked about some detail of a crime (such as the colour of a wallet) which only a guilty person would know: only a guilty person would show increased signed of anxiety. In the *control question technique* reactions to neutral questions are compared to reactions to key questions such as 'did you steal anything in your last job?'

Determining the accuracy of lie detectors is particularly difficult. It is hard to set up controlled experiments or surveys. There is also the problem that lie detectors can be 100 per cent accurate in detecting guilty people by accusing *all* suspects of telling lies. The accuracy is bought at the expense of making false accusations against the majority of innocent people. Indeed, this large number of false positives is one of the aspects of lie detectors which has received greatest criticism.

There is quite a lot of evidence that lie detectors do not work and that in situations where they seem to work, the success is due to other factors. For example, in one experiment some subjects were induced to cheat at a maths test and then all the candidates were subjected to a lie detector test. For a part of the sample, the interrogators were given only the *results* from the polygraph and in these cases they had only chance success. For another part of the sample the interrogator was only allowed to *observe* the subject under polygraph questioning. In the third part of the sample the interrogator was allowed to *observe and inspect* the polygraph records. The last two groups produced equal, above chance detection rates. The results of this experiment suggest that it is the observable behaviour of those undergoing polygraph examination, not the polygraph records, that is the crucial factor. A further problem is that people can train themselves to combat the polygraph by evoking emotional responses to all questions (e.g. by biting one's lip or thinking of a guilty secret when answering *all* questions).

On the basis of these considerations a working party of the British Psychological Society came to the conclusion that 'it is difficult to see how members of the society could engage in work as polygraph interrogators and claim that their conduct is compatible with the Society's current code of conduct'. In 1988 President Reagan signed a law banning the use of polygraphs for pre-employment screening.

Honesty tests

It has been claimed that theft by employees is the largest source of criminal loss against business. One American survey suggests that 26 per cent of employees in manufacturing, 32 per cent of hospital employees and 41 per cent of employees in the retail sector have engaged in theft from their employers. In response to figures such as these a growing number of employers are attempting to detect, at the selection stage, those candidates who are most likely to engage in these activities.

In response to this demand a number of questionnaires has been developed. The questionnaires adopt one of two main approaches. First, there are questionnaires which ask candidates if they have engaged in certain activities: for example, 'Have you ever stolen anything worth more than £5 from a previous employer?' or 'Have you ever had a conviction for theft?' Second, there are questionnaires which ask about candidates' opinions concerning dishonest practices, e.g., 'Should a person be fired if caught stealing from an employer?' or, 'What percentage of people take more than £1 per week from their employer?'

Considering that honesty testing is a fairly new development, there is surprisingly plentiful evidence about how good they are. Sackett and Harris reviewed studies of ten different tests. One study, for example, looked at workers collecting donations for charities. It was found that those selected by the test collected, on average, $18 per day more than those with lower scores. In another example, those who were ultimately dismissed from a department store for theft and other offences had significantly lower scores. Sackett and Harris argue a case that compelling evidence of the validity of honesty tests has not yet been produced, but they also note that what stands out is the consistency of positive findings across tests and across validation situations. They also indicate that there seem to be few equal opportunity implications for these types of test.

Particularly good information is available concerning one test, the Personnel Selection Inventory Dishonesty Scale. It is a scale which attempts to measure three aspects of undesirable behaviours: dishonesty, violence and emotional instability, and alcohol and drug use. A meta-analysis of a combined sample of 1806 applicants conducted by McDaniel and Jones indicates that the dishonesty scale has a validity of 0.5. This is probably an overestimate of the scale's validity in operational settings since some of the subject were students and the replies were anonymous. Furthermore, in some cases the subjects knew that independent evidence of their honesty was available. From the data supplied by McDaniel and Jones, it would appear that when these influences are taken into account the validity would be about 0.33.

Accomplishment records

Accomplishment records require considerable preparation. First the job is analysed to determine the key areas of job performance. Then a simple form is drawn up and candidates are asked to state their previous accomplishments in each of the key areas. Finally, the statements are scored according to a carefully developed rating scale which gives specific examples of accomplishments at different levels (BARS). Initial results indicate that the method is highly reliable, and validity correlations of 0.25–0.47 were obtained against subsequent performance. Hunter and Hunter's meta-analysis indicates that the validity of such behavioural consistency approaches is 0.49.

Future autobiographies

Most methods of selection use either past performance such as experience, or current performance, such as tests, to predict *future performance*. It is probably apposite to end this chapter by briefly describing one measure which also looks into the future.

It starts with a notion long held in careers psychology: we all have some idea of what we would ideally like to be and that our lives are a process of moving from what we are now to what we would like to be. In technical terms, human endeavour is a process of implementing our ideal selves. It follows that if we want to know how someone will behave in the future we need to find out what ideals they hold for themselves. Perhaps the best example of future autobiographies is the work by Tullar and Barrett.

Salesmen were asked to write a future autobiography stating what they would be doing five years from that date. The future autobiographies were then scored on three dimensions which had emerged out of work selecting Peace Corps volunteers. The three dimensions were: (1) the extent to which he saw himself as the main *determinant of his future;* (2) the extent to which he saw life as a series of *long term demands* requiring effort; and (3) the extent to which he had a detailed and *complex view of the future*. The ratings were then correlated with performance judgements provided by the salesmen's district managers.

The results suggest that the ratings of complexity were not particularly good and provided correlations of about 0.17. However, ratings for demand and self determination seemed to offer some promise and yielded correlations of about 0.26 and 0.39, respectively. Such correlations are not particularly high and they are based on a tiny sample. But, they may well be particularly important because they may measure aspects which are not covered by other methods of selection.

Further reading

Ben-Shakhar, G., Bar-Hillel, M., Bilu, Y., Ben-Abba, E. and Flug, A. (1986) 'Can graphology predict occupational success? Two empirical studies and some methodological ruminations', *Journal of Applied Psychology*, 71, **4**, 645–53.

British Psychological Society (1986) 'Report of the working party on the use of the polygraph in criminal investigation and personnel screening', *Bulletin of the British Psychological Society*, 39, 81–94.

Camara, W. J. (1988) 'Reagan signs ban of polygraph testing for job applicants', *The Industrial-Organisational Psychologist*, 26, **1**, 39–41.

Eysenck, H. J. and Nias, D. K. B. (1982) *Astrology: Science or Superstition?*, London, Maurice Temple Smith.

George, D. I. and Smith, M. C. (1988) 'Self assessment in personnel selection: an investigation using seasonal workers', *Applied Psychology: an International Review*, 37, **4**, 337–50.

Hough, L. M. (1984) 'Development and evaluation of the "Accomplishment Record" method of selecting and promoting professionals', *Journal of Applied Psychology*, 69, **1**, 135–46.

Klimoski, R. J. and Rafaeli, A. (1983) 'Inferring personal qualities through handwriting analysis', *Journal of Occupational Psychology*, 56, 191–202.

McDaniel, M. A. and Jones, J. W. (1986) 'A meta analysis of the validity of the employee attitude inventory theft scales', *Journal of Business and Psychology*, 1, **1**, 31–50.

McKenzie Davey, D. and Harris, M. (eds.) (1982) *Judging People: A guide to orthodox and unorthodox methods of assessment*, London, Mcgraw-Hill.

Reilly, R. R. and Chao, G. T. (1982) 'Validity and fairness of some alternative employee selection procedures', *Personnel Psychology*, 35, 1–83.

Sackett, P. R. and Harris, M. M. (1984) 'Honesty testing for personnel selection: A review and critique', *Personnel Psychology*, 37, 221–46.

Tuller, W. L. and Barrett, G. V. (1976) 'The future autobiography as a predictor of sales success', *Journal of Applied Psychology*, 61, **3**, 371–3.

Tyson, G. A. (1982) 'Why people perceive horoscopes as being true', *Bulletin of the British Psychological Society*, 35, 186–8.

8 Bias in selection

Discrimination is the essence of good selection: the employer is trying to discriminate between those who will turn out to be good employees and those who will turn out to be poor ones. In part, the success of an organisation depends on making this discrimination accurately, as otherwise the organisation fails and its employees lose their jobs. Proper discrimination is also important from the viewpoint of the individual: it is galling for an individual to learn that a job has been awarded to a less able candidate. The less able candidate may also be in for an emotionally draining time as he or she discovers that they are out of their depth in their new job.

However, this discrimination must be based upon the ability to perform the job. In practically all circumstances, the discrimination should not be based on the applicant's race, sex, age or disability. When the selection decision is based on any of these factors it is usually termed bias.

Concern over the potential bias of selection methods rose to a height during the 1970s as equal opportunity legislation began to bite. In the immediate firing line were psychological tests, probably because test scores are quantitative and it is easiest to show bias where clear scores are recorded. The initial reaction of many organisations in the USA was to abandon the use of tests and place greater reliance on interviews. One psychologist commented that this was equivalent to the rats swimming towards a sinking ship. Ironically, the scope for bias in an interview is probably greater than in any other selection device, but because interviews are often muddled and subjective the bias may be harder to prove.

With the immense benefit of hindsight we can now see that

many of the concerns about bias in selection were misguided. Since the 1970s we have clarified our ideas as to what constitutes bias and we have reasonably clear estimates of the degree of bias produced by various methods of selection. In general, it is possible to conclude that bias is less frequent than we once thought and consequently attention has turned to the possibilities of bias at the job analysis and recruitment stages.

What is bias?

Much of the original concern over bias in selection was due to muddled thinking about what constituted bias.

Initially, evidence seemed to be based on the *opinions of rejected applicants*. This type of evidence can be dismissed after only a little thought: rejected applicants may merely be rationalising their experiences to maintain their pride. At a more cynical level some rejected applicants might claim bias as a political ploy in order to gain some personal advantage. Reports of rejected applicants are worthwhile only when they relate to specific irregularities which have some form of independent corroboration.

Expert opinion has also proved to be a very inadequate type of evidence of bias. In one particular case the author of one very well established test of intelligence, David Wechsler, gave the opinion on TV that certain questions in his tests were biased against 'black' children. Unfortunately, later empirical data showed that, if anything, black children tended to give right answers to these questions slightly more often than white children. This anecdotal evidence is supported by carefully designed studies. In one study, 100 people were asked to judge the bias in 30 questions. The judges were taken from three ethnic groups: Hispanic, black and white Americans. Half of the 30 questions were known to be biased against non-white Americans, but neither the Hispanic group, nor the black group nor the white group had above chance success in identifying which questions these were. The final nail in this particular coffin of expert opinion was another study in which black experts, who either had PhDs in psychology or were advanced graduate students, were asked to judge the bias of items in a test. Again the results were little better than chance.

The clear conclusion which emerges so far is that someone's opinion of what is fair and what is biased is worth very little indeed. Consequently the search for evidence began elsewhere and one of the more promising areas seemed to be *the proportions engaged*.

The rationale for using the proportions engaged is alluringly direct. If a minority group represents 20 per cent of a population, then surely under an unbiased selection system 20 per cent of employees in any given job should be of that minority group. This type of rationale is embedded in many reports which are published by equal opportunity agencies. This rationale led to the 4/5 rule contained in the USA's *Uniform Guidelines on Employee Selection Procedures*. In essence, these guidelines imply that bias exists if the hiring rate for a minority group drops below 4/5 the hiring rate of the majority group. For example, if a firm employs 50 out of every hundred men who apply and employs only 39 out of every hundred women who apply it would amount to bias under the 4/5 rule.

The 4/5 rule had its heyday in the US courts in the 1970s but its influence has since declined. The problem with the 4/5 rule is that it is based on the *assumption* that all groups are, on average, equal in all things in all localities at all times. This assumption is clearly untenable. We know that the characteristics of groups do vary (but not necessarily in a way that is to the majority group's advantage). For example, an expanding company might have five vacancies for inspectors in its quality control department. An advert in the local press produced applications from 100 women and applications from 20 men. Despite its enthusiasm for an equal opportunities policy the company found itself offering all five places to men. Contrary to superficial appearances, there was no bias. Local circumstances had conspired to produce a situation in which the levels of suitability of the men and women applicants were not equal. Two firms in the locality had gone bankrupt. One was a small engineering firm producing similar products and employing five experienced inspectors. The other bankrupt firm was a large knitting company employing a large number of women lockstitchers. Out of desperation, practically all the redundant workers applied for the five new inspection jobs. Quite sensibly the firm chose the experienced workers – who coincidentally happened to be men.

Considerations such as these mean that the proportions engaged can never provide unequivocal evidence of bias. However, the weaknesses of this type of evidence need to be seen in context. Any employer who employs noticeably lower proportions of minority groups should pause for thought and examine existing procedures to see if they are biased against minority groups. This is particularly true of large organisations recruiting large numbers of employees in many different localities.

The only really conclusive way of establishing bias is to *compare the scores which are obtained at the selection stage with subsequent performance* on the job. If a selection method is biased, it will tend to underestimate the performance of a minority group. This approach is rarely discussed in the press because it is inherently a method which requires considerable statistical nous. The following simplified example will give some idea of the principles involved.

Suppose a company uses a test to select 20 widget makers and that the test produces a score from 1–10. Three months after training it checks on the performance of the employees by working out the average number of widgets made per hour over, say, a four-week period. By coincidence the average number of widgets also ranges from 1–10. The company then casts the results into a scattergram similar to those described in Chapter 1. A trend line is then drawn through the points to represent the relationship between the selection score and subsequent performance. This trend line can be gauged by eye or, preferably, derived from a regression formula. This line represents the predictions which are implicitly made on the basis of the selection method. Of course, no method of selection is perfect and only a few people perform exactly as predicted and have points which lie exactly on the trend line. The distance from the trend line represents error.

Bias exists when the error works in one direction for the majority group and in another direction for the minority group.

Figure 8.1a shows how a scattergram for 20 employees might appear.

Visual inspection of Figure 8.1 suggests that the squares have a slight tendency to appear above the line whilst the rounds tend to appear below the line. The exact level of bias can be obtained by measuring the distances for each subgroup from the trend line as shown in Figure 8.1b (in actual fact these distances are then squared) and then the average distance for

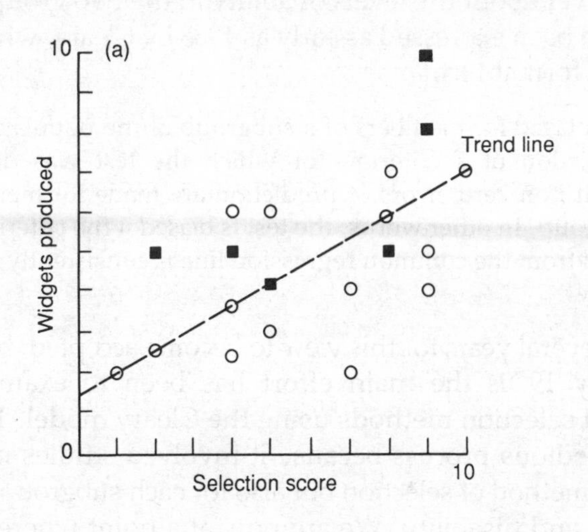

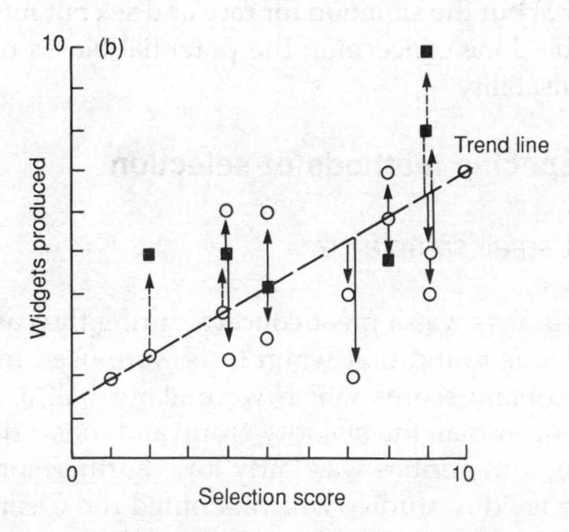

8.1 Regression method of proving bias

each group is found. The size of the sample is an important consideration because with small samples of about 20–30 there is a large variation due to chance factors. Consequently sample size must be taken into account when judging the significance of any differences which do emerge. If a significant difference between the two averages is found then we can be fairly sure that some form of bias exists. It should be noted that this method is objective, quantifiable, and makes no assumption whatsoever about the levels of ability in the two groups. This view had been expressed as early as 1968 by Cleary, who wrote in more formal terms:

> A test is biased for members of a subgroup of the population if, in the prediction of a criterion for which the test was designed, consistent non-zero errors of prediction are made for members of the subgroup. In other words, the test is biased if the criterion score predicted from the common regression line is consistently too high or too low.

It took several years for this view to become accepted, but since the early 1970s the main effort has been to examine the different selection methods using the Cleary model. This has been a tedious process because it involved studies not only on each method of selection but also for each subgroup of race, sex, age and disability. We are now at a point where we are fairly clear about the situation for race and sex but much work needs to be done concerning the potential biases regarding age and disability.

Bias of specific methods of selection

Impact of small sample size

Racial bias in tests was a great concern during the early 1970s because it was found that when tests were used minorities tended to obtain scores which were about half a standard deviation lower than the majority group and consequently the hiring rate of minorities was fairly low. Furthermore, about half of the validity studies which adopted the Cleary model also found significant differences. Consequently, many people concluded that tests were biased. Subsequent work has overturned this conclusion. As noted above, average marks and hiring rates are not conclusive evidence of bias because they make the assumption that ability in the two groups is exactly equal. However, the findings from the validity studies seemed to offer a more substantive evidence. A classic study by Boem, which has been replicated by at least three other workers, suggested that the conclusion of differential validity was due to statistical artifacts caused by low sample sizes. In essence, she found that the sample sizes of whites in such studies were reasonably large, say between 50 and 100, and that the average distance from the prediction line based on these samples was reasonably stable. However, the sample size for blacks in these studies was often tiny, say less than 30, and the average distance from the prediction line was very unstable. It was this statistical instability in the averages for the blacks which was producing the differential validity in about half of the studies. When larger samples or less crude methods of analysis were used tests generally emerged as fair to both groups. In 1980 it was firmly concluded that differential validity of tests was a non-existent phenomenon.

Sex bias of tests has attracted less research attention, but there seems to be a consistent finding that it is easier to predict, for good or bad, the subsequent performance of women – but this in itself does not amount to bias one way or the other. It also seems that women consistently obtain scores on *physical tests* which on average are about one standard deviation below the average for men. There are relatively few studies using the more definitive Cleary model and often even these studies are concerned with academic institutions. Therefore, only a tentative conclusion can be drawn that tests have a small but statistically significant bias in favour of women.

Bias of interviews

On a prima facie basis interviews have great scope for bias because they almost always allow considerable room for subjectivity. However, as the first chapter in this book points out, interviews are generally little better than chance at selecting good employees and chance is equally fair and equally inaccurate to all groups. The evidence from careful studies tends to confirm this conclusion as far as racial subgroups are concerned – indeed recent studies from the USA suggest that if interviews are biased in any way then there is a small bias in favour of minority groups. However, this conclusion needs to be interpreted with great care: it could be a reflection of policies of affirmative action or it could result from statistical error. The situation in respect of the bias of interviews towards women is slightly more complex. Generally, it would seem that interviews are not biased against women but this conclusion may need to be modified in certain situations. If a woman is applying for work in an occupation which is traditionally viewed as men's work and where the majority of present workers are men, there is some evidence that interviews are moderately biased against women.

Bias of other methods of selection

Schmitt in 1986 reviewed most of the studies of methods of selection and equality of opportunity. In brief his conclusions, based mainly on data from the USA, were:

- *Assessment centres* do not adversely affect the *hiring* rate of minority group individuals, and *promotion* decisions based upon an assessment centre do not differ according to the race and sex of the assessment centre participants.
- *Work samples* have the potential for bias when the performance on the work sample is *rated* rather than measuring what is actually produced.
- *Biodata* poses many issues relevant to equality of opportunity since many items such as economic standing, area of residence, educational or social experiences, etc. may be a reflection of racial or sex membership, and consequently there is the possibility of considerable bias. This possibility can be minimised by using only those biodata items which have been shown by a job analysis to be directly related to work. Schmitt also makes the point that it is difficult to arrive at any definitive conclusion about the fairness of

biodata methods because there is insufficient work using the methods outlined by Cleary.

- *Peer evaluations* have attracted very little research attention, but one study found no race effect in a group in which there were roughly equal proportions of minority and majority racial groups. What is really needed though, are studies in more typical situations where the minority group is, in fact, in a minority.
- *Data concerning age bias is almost non existent,* but there is a myriad of studies examining the relationship between age and performance. The general outcome of these studies is two-fold. First, age stereotypes exist and supervisors tend to give lower ratings to older workers. Second, older workers tend to produce more than younger ones. However, this last conclusion needs some differentiation. There is some evidence that performance tends to increase with age in professional jobs but performance tends to decrease with age in non-professional work.

In an effort to present a clear outline of the main results the previous sections have avoided reference to two major complications which must be borne in mind whenever studies of bias in selection are planned or interpreted. They are the criteria issues and the issue of international generalisability.

Criteria in studies of bias

Many of the studies outlined above have failed to show any large degree of bias. This could arise from a very simple artifact. If both a selection method and the method of evaluating performance are equally biased, then according to the Cleary method all would *seem* fair. An example will make the situation clearer. Suppose there were a set of interviews which were biased against minority applicants by, say, one point on a 10-point scale. The company then does a validity study with 200 majority group employees and 100 minority group employees. Because of the nature of the job it is impossible to use production records, so supervisors are asked to rate the workers on a 10-point scale. If these supervisory ratings are also biased against minority applicants by one point the regression line on the graph in Figure 8.1 would predict the ratings very accurately and all would seem fair because the two sets of biases would, statistically, cancel each other out.

Criticisms of this kind were taken very seriously and investigated by several researchers. In particular, they compared the biases of selection methods using soft, subjective criteria such as supervisors' ratings, and the biases of selection methods using hard, objective criteria such as the actual number of widgets produced. Two major reviews of this problem covered 74 and 53 studies respectively. The general conclusion seems to be that subjective indices closely mirror the objective indices and that this cannot be a major explanation of why little bias in selection is found to exist.

International differences in studies of bias

Almost all of the studies on which this chapter is based are from the USA, and the question arises whether the same findings are true in other countries. The answer may well depend upon the focus of the study. The findings concerning sex discrimination are probably universal since women in most countries comprise rather more than 50 per cent of the population and are also indigenous to that country.

The situation in respect to racial groups may be rather different as a comparison between the USA and the UK will show. The black population of the USA has existed for many generations, arisen largely out of enforced slavery, predominantly from Africa and accounting for about 18 per cent of the population. In the UK the situation is very different. The black population has a history on average of two generations, was the result of voluntary immigration from three continents and comprises about 5 per cent of the population. Such intrinsic differences have had an impact on the timing, nature and enforcement of legislation and attitudes which *might* give rise to differing results. What is more, the relatively small number of black people in the population means that it is extraordinarily difficult to obtain samples of sufficient size in order to obtain conclusive evidence of bias.

Affirmative action and productivity

In the USA there has been on-going consideration of the effects of affirmative action programmes on national productivity. A typical affirmative action programme consists of target quotas for proportions of minority groups, and sometimes these are enforced by methods of contract compliance. A classic study by Hunter examined the economic impact of hiring solely on merit using a range of selection methods and hiring using a quota method. Using the methods of utility analysis to be described in the next chapter it is possible to work out that for a company operating in an area where one in 10 of the population belongs to the minority group, where there are 10 applicants for every job which has a salary of 20,000 ecus per year, and where there are 100 posts to be filled, the operation of a quota system would cost the firm over a million ecus per year in terms of lost productivity.

Of course, this is an over-simplification because many other factors need to be taken into account – for example, there is a tendency for minority group applicants to drop out if the selection procedure is drawn out, and this has the effect of undoing some of the quota system. However, calculations of this kind are useful in pointing out that affirmative action programmes have costs to their organisations and the communities in which these organisations exist but, to paraphrase Schmitt, how to equate economic aspects with social and political concerns about reverse discrimination or the obligation to right past discriminations is a much more difficult problem.

Further reading

Probably the best single reference is:

Schmitt, N. and Noe, R. A. (1986) 'Personnel selection and equal employment opportunity' in Cooper, C. L. and Robertson, I. T. (eds) *Review of Industrial and Organisational Psychology*, Chichester, Wiley.

Important and classic papers are:

Boem, V. R. (1972) 'Negro–white differences in validity of employment and training procedures', *Journal of Applied Psychology*, 56, 33–9.

Hunter, J. E., Schmidt, F. L. and Rauschenberger, J. K. (1977) 'Fairness of psychological tests: implications of four definitions of selection utility and minority hiring', *Journal of Applied Psychology*, 62, 245–60.

Reilly, R. S. and Chao, G. T. (1982) 'Validity and fairness of some alternative employee selection procedures', *Personnel Psychology*, 35, 1–55.

A statistical masochist may care to struggle with:

Cleary, T. A. and Hilton, T. L. (1968) 'An investigation into item bias', *Educational and Psychological Measurement*, 28, 61–75.

For a British perspective:

Pearn, M. A. (1989) 'Fairness in employee selection: a comparison of UK and USA experience', in Smith, J. M. and Robertson, I. T. (eds) *Advances in Selection and Assessment*, Chichester, Wiley.

Probably the most comprehensive book on the statistical aspects of bias in testing, which is general and is not focused on employee selection is:

Jensen, A. R. (1980) *Bias in Mental Testing*, London, Methuen.

9 Calculating the cash benefits of selection

Importance of cash values to decision makers

In most organisations there are never enough cash resources to meet all the demands. A production manager may want 200,000 ecus to install a new 'just in time' production system, the marketing manager may want a similar sum for a press launch, and a personnel manager may want the 200,000 ecus to overhaul the organisation's selection methods. In this scramble for funds, it is usually the personnel manager who loses out. The reason is painfully clear. The production manager will be able to show that the 'just in time' system will lower inventory costs by 500,000 ecus. The marketing manager will estimate new sales to have a cash value of, say, half a million ecus. The hapless personnel manager will argue a case that investment in selection is generally a 'good thing'. Organisational decision makers are used to dealing in arguments couched in money terms. More often than not, the lion's share of resources goes to those functions who can present their case in cash terms. More often than not the personnel department loses out.

In the last decade, great strides have been made in working out the cash value of selection. These developments are generally known under the heading of *utility analysis*. In almost all cases investment in selection procedures has been shown to be one of the best investments an organisation can make. Furthermore, utility analysis has now developed to the point where different strategies of selection can be compared and an informed choice of the most effective strategy can be taken. Indeed, these developments are making personnel managers into managers of human resources in the same hard-nosed, quantitative way that finance managers are managers of financial resources.

The Brogden-Hunter method of calculating utility

The work on Utility Theory was started in the 1950s and 1960s by Brogden but it remained a theoretical development until practical applications were identified by Jack Hunter and Frank Schmidt. The method proceeds in five main stages. For the purposes of explanation we will imagine the calculations as applied to the selection of salesmen who earn on average 20,000 ecus per year.

Stage 1: Selection at random. The first stage is to work out what would happen if selectors worked at random choosing employees with a pin. Elementary laws of statistics predict that the output of a group of workers would form a normal, bell-shaped distribution, as shown in Figure 9.1, in which most salesmen would produce sales to the value of about 20,000 ecus, with a few producing much smaller sales and a few much

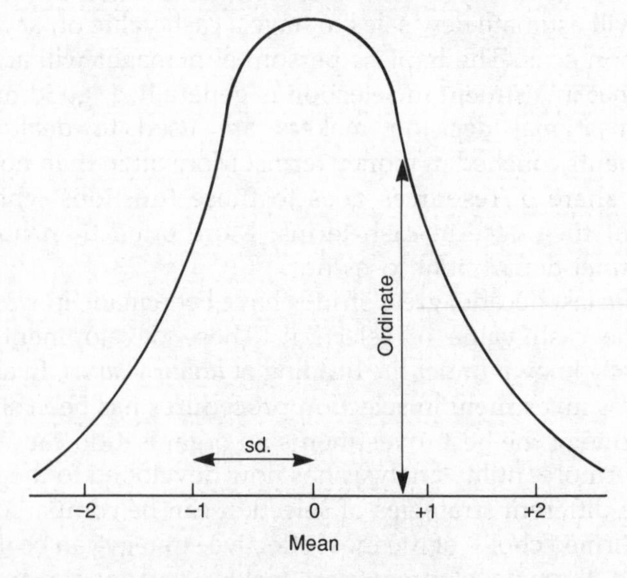

9.1 Selection at random

larger sales. Most human characteristics such as height, intelligence and personality produce this normal distribution and there is a lot of empirical evidence to show that worker productivity also follows the bell-shaped pattern. Elementary statistics show that in order to describe the normal distribution two parameters are needed – the central point of the distribution (*the mean*) and a measure of spread (*the standard deviation, the sd*). The height of the curve at any given point on the bottom axis is known as the *ordinate*.

Stage 2: Perfect selection. The second stage is to work out what would happen if we were able to select employees with perfect accuracy. A lot depends on the selection ratio. If there are 10 applicants to every job the selection ratio is 0.1; if there are five applicants to every job the selection ratio is 0.2; and if there are three applicants to every job the selection ratio is 0.33.

Obviously, if we were able to select with perfect accuracy we would select from the extreme right of the normal curve, i.e. if we had a selection ratio of 0.33 we would select the top third of the distribution – the shaded part of Figure 9.2.

Statistics tables can be used to tell us where to draw the

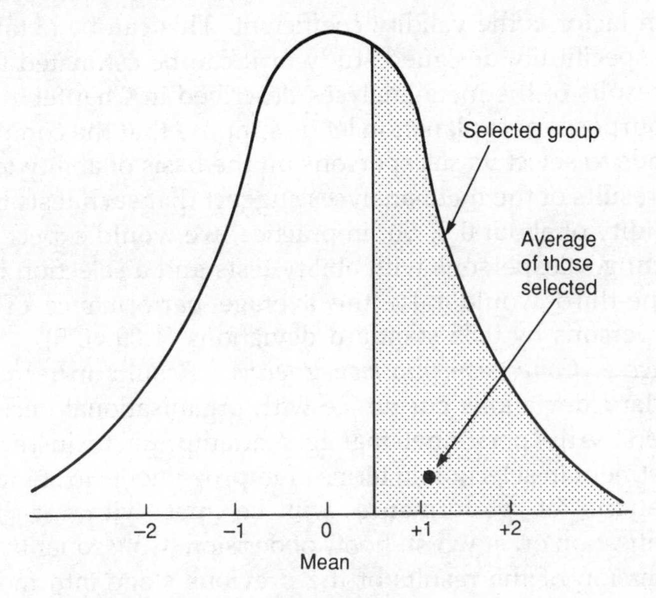

9.2 Perfect selection

borderline between accepts and rejects. For example, the table at the end of this chapter shows that for a selection ratio of 0.33 we would need to draw the diving line 0.44 standard deviations above the mean and that the ordinate at this point is 0.36.

The question arises, 'what is the average performance of those people in the shaded area (the selectees)?' This could be answered by drawing the diagram on graph paper and counting squares. This process is tedious, error-prone and inaccurate. It is better to calculate the average productivity using the formula:

$$\text{average performance} = \frac{\text{ordinate}}{\text{selection ratio}}$$

Thus, if the selection ratio is one-third and we can choose with perfect accuracy, the average output of the employees we select will be 1.09 standard deviations above average (0.36/0.33).

Stage 3: Selection in practice. It is patently obvious that we can never select with perfect accuracy. The figure obtained in the previous stage is the theoretical maximum. It needs to be scaled down in order to conform to reality. The scaling down factor is the validity coefficient. This can be obtained by a specifically designed study or it can be estimated from the results of the meta-analyses described in Chapter 1. For the purposes of explanation let us suppose that the company intends to select its salespersons on the basis of ability tests. The results of the meta-analyses suggest that such tests have a validity of about 0.5. So, in practice, we would expect that selecting salespersons with ability tests and a selection ratio of one-third would raise the average performance of the salespersons by 0.55 standard deviations (1.09×0.5).

Stage 4: Conversion into money terms. Results in terms of standard deviations cut no ice with organisational decision makers. Any personnel manager attempting to justify an investment in selection in terms of improvements in standard deviations of performance will be met with, at best, mystification or, at worst, hoots of derision. Consequently the conversion of the results of the previous stage into money terms is a crucial step and it all hangs on the question, 'How much is a standard deviation worth?' This question can be answered in three ways.

First, the accounts department can be asked to cost the output of a sample of 50–100 incumbents and the standard deviation can be computed. In essence, this involves working out the resources in terms of materials and overheads consumed by each worker in the sample and subtracting this from the value of his or her finished product. In the case of some operative occupations where there is a standard product whose market value is known this may be a feasible approach. However, in many jobs, especially professional or managerial jobs, establishing the value of the finished product may be almost impossible. Furthermore, this method cannot be used when there are only a few incumbents in the job in question. This method is rarely attempted.

A *second* way of establishing the cash value of the standard deviation of performance is to ask experts to judge the value. Typically, a group of ten or a dozen supervisors are asked to estimate the value of an average worker (50th percentile). Next they are asked to estimate the value of the work of a good worker – one who is better than 85 per cent of workers. Finally, they are asked to estimate the value of a poor worker – who is worse than 85 per cent of workers. The consensus figures for all the supervisors in the sample are calculated. As it happens, the 85th percentile is almost exactly one standard deviation from the mean, so it is easy to use the three estimates (mean, top 85 per cent and bottom 85 per cent) to calculate the money value of a standard deviation of performance. Even this procedure is time-consuming and there may not be enough supervisors available to form an acceptable sample of judges to make the estimates.

A *third* way of estimating the money value of the standard deviation of performance is the 40 per cent rule. It was noticed that when the other methods were used they tended to give a figure which was 40 per cent of the wages paid. Thus it seems reasonable to adopt this ratio as a general rule of thumb. Consequently, if a salesperson is earning £10,000 per year, the money value of the standard deviation of performance is likely to be about £4,000.

Once the value of the standard deviation of performance has been established it is easy to convert the improvement in standard deviation terms into an improvement in money terms. In our example the improvement in sd terms was 0.55. Consequently, the improvement in money terms will be 4,364 ecus per year (8000×0.55).

Stage 5: Value per workgroup. Individuals rarely stay with an organisation for exactly one year and selection systems are rarely used on just one person. The calculations need to be adjusted to reflect these facts. In our example, the average salesperson stays with the organisation for 1.5 years and the selection system is used to select 10 salespersons. This means that the improvement in money terms is 6,546 ecus per individual or 65,454 ecus for all 10 salespeople (1.5×4,364).

Stage 6: Taking costs into account. Selection systems do not appear out of thin air nor are they given free by test publishers and consultants. The processes of selection also consume the time of the personnel department, and the expenses paid to applicants can mount up to a king's ransom. All of this must be set against the benefits. In the hypothetical example these costs may well come to 600 ecus per candidate and it was necessary to screen 30 applicants in order to obtain 10 successful ones. The total costs of 18,000 ecus must be subtracted from the benefit to reveal a net benefit of 47,454 ecus.

For most purposes the figure produced at the end of stage 5 will be quite adequate since it will be comparable to the estimates bandied around by other functions as they make their bids for resources. It can form the basis for further calculation of the ratios such as 'rate of return on capital' or 'payback period', which decision makers often use when allocating resources.

However, two notes of caution are needed: this method of calculation is not appropriate in certain circumstances and, in fact, the calculations need to be refined further.

The Taylor-Russell approach

The method developed by Brogden and Hunter is probably the most frequently used method of analysing the utility of a selection system, but it has one major disadvantage. It assumes a continuum of performance and that an individual's position on that continuum is determined by their abilities and motivation. However, there are many jobs where this is not so: one is either a competent policeman or one is not a competent policeman; one is either able to keep up with a production line at a certain quality of work or one is not. In situations of this kind the Brodgen-Hunter method cannot be used. Instead, the Taylor-Russell approach is more appropriate.

In some senses the Taylor-Russell approach is easier to use and it requires information on three main parameters.

- The selection ratio which is exactly the same as the sr used in the Brogden-Hunter method.
- The validity coefficient which is also the same as the validity coefficient used in the Brogden-Hunter method.
- The percentage of applicants who can adequately perform the job. This is an indirect measure of the job's level of difficulty. Only about 30 per cent of applicants chosen at random may be able to do a difficult job while, say, 80 per cent may be able to do an easy job. In practice the percentage of applicants able to do a job should be ascertained empirically or an estimate should be made on some systematic basis.

The Russell-Taylor method integrates this information using a complex formula and it estimates the percentage of selected applicants who will be able to do the job. Unfortunately, these calculations are complex. However, Lawshe and co-workers constructed a series of tables which can be used to circumvent the actual calculations. A version of these tables is given at the end of this chapter.

Specific examples of utility analysis

Utility analysis has been applied to many occupations and the almost invariable conclusion is that selection is one of the most cost-effective investments any organisation can make. In 1972 Lee and Booth estimated that using a weighted application blank (see Chapter 5 concerning biodata) to select 245 clerical workers in a situation where about one in four applicants were offered a job would save the organisation $249,946. A decade later, investigators led by Arnold showed that using a dynamometer to measure the maximum pull which an applicant for a labouring job in a steel company could exert with their arms would save the steel company approximately nine million dollars a year if the dynamometer were used to select its average intake of 1,853 labourers per year.

The savings are equally great when effective selection methods are used with managerial and professional workers. In 1982 a group of researchers led by Frank Schmidt showed that by using a relatively simple pencil and paper test to select computer programmers, the government of the USA could save as much as $97,200,000. In this particular case the employer hired about 618 new programmers per year and had twenty applicants for each job. Once hired, the employees tended to stay with the organisation a very long time (about nine years). A final example is the work of Casio and Silbey. They conducted a utility analysis of the promotion of sales managers in which the interview was replaced by an assessment centre. Even though assessment centres are one of the most expensive methods of selection and the selection ratio was poor (one in two aspirants were promoted) and the number of promotions was not high (about 50), the savings to the organisation were still large – $154,004.

Refining the utility estimates

The huge savings indicated by utility analyses are probably an overestimate. John Boudreau points out they need to be adjusted for three additional factors which may have a marked effect on the result of the calculation – perhaps reducing it by 80 per cent. These additional factors need to be handled with care. They apply to all investments an organsiation can make and it would be stupid and unfair for the personnel function to include them when functions such as production and data processing do not include them in theirs. The three additional factors are variable costs, inflation and taxes.

Variable costs need to be taken into account because good workers generally incur more expenditure than poor workers. This is most clearly seen in the case of sales representatives. A good representative will spend more time 'on the road' and will therefore have higher travel claims. He or she will use more brochures and the extra business that is generated will probably mean that a higher level of stocks needs to be maintained. These extra costs must be subtracted from the extra sales revenue that a good representative achieves. The same considerations apply to most categories of worker.

Inflation must also be taken into account. Most selection costs are 'upfront' at the point of engagement, whilst the benefits of having a more able workforce accumulate over a number of years. Inflation means that today's money is almost certain to be worth several percentage points more than tomorrow's money.

Most organisations pay *tax*. Consequently the government will cream off a slice of any benefit. However, organisations which are exempt from tax should note the implications of tax exemption – because some of the benefit is not syphoned off, good selection is particularly cost-effective in organsiations which do not pay tax.

The calculation of these effects is not particularly new and if they need to be taken into account the financial department in most organisations can be asked to provide the appropriate expertise.

Utility analysis and human resource management

Perhaps one of the most exciting prospects is the role which utility analysis will have in enabling the personnel function to manage an organisation's human resources more effectively. At present personnel managers have to make all sorts of essentially subjective decisions. Faced with a decision on how to use a windfall budget allocation of £50,000, how does a personnel manager decide between the many possible options, such as a wider advertising campaign for operatives, the introduction of situational interviews for clerical staff, or establishing assessment centres for management? Utility analysis can be used to guide these decisions in a quantitative way.

For example, Boudreau and Rynes looked at a decision which might face one organisation: should they spend money developing an advertising campaign and a biodata key which could be used to score application forms or should they employ a recruitment agency and then interview those who were put forward? Both strategies have advantages and disadvantages. Press advertising is likely to attract a lot of only moderately suitable candidates but screening application forms is quite a good method of selection. The recruitment agency, on the other hand, seems likely to attract a better pool of candidates, but the interview is a poor way of selecting among those put forward. Faced with this choice a personnel manager must usually rely on their intuition and experience and like all human intuition and experience this can be very subjective. Utility analysis can be used to work out the costs and benefits so that an informed decision can be made. In the particular circumstances envisaged by Boudreau and Rynes the use of the recruitment agency appeared to be the superior strategy. In practice, the utility of other combinations would need to be examined.

Utility analysis can be used to work out the sensitivity or the robustness of various recruitment strategies. Many decisions need to be made in anticipation of the future and often the future does not conform to expectations. Utility analysis can be used to see how easily a selection strategy can be blown off course. For example, a company may design a selection system on the assumption that the labour market remains fairly favourable and that they can achieve a selection ratio of four applicants for every job. However, labour markets can change so the organisation repeats the calculations assuming an improvement in the labour market to, say, one in six, and it also repeats the calculations assuming a deteriorating market where it will need to accept one out of every two applicants. If necessary it could also vary the expected length of service or the numbers likely to be recruited. In this way decision making can become very sophisticated and the company may not choose the selection method or strategy which yields the highest value; instead it may choose the selection strategy which produces the surest results.

A final implication needs to be noted. The methods of utility analysis are beginning to be applied to other personnel techniques such as training, participation and incentive schemes. The available data does not allow any firm comparisons to be drawn. But, looking towards the horizon, there are indications that selection is one of the most cost-effective techniques available to personnel functions.

Statistical tables for use in utility calculations

These tables are those most frequently needed in utility calculations and they are abstracted from more comprehensive ones. The ordinates of the normal curve are abstracted from Guilford, J. P., (1965) *Fundamental Statistics in Psychology and Education*, New York, Mcgraw-Hill, but equivalent tables are available in most good statistics texts. The expectancy tables are extracted from those reproduced by Smith, J. M. and Robertson, I. T. (1986) *The Theory and Practice of Systematic Staff Selection*, London, Macmillan.

Ordinates of the normal curve

Standard score	*Selection ratio*	*Ordinate*
2.32	1/100	0.027
2.05	1/50	0.049
1.64	1/20	0.104
1.29	1/10	0.174
1.15	1/8	0.206
1.06	1/7	0.228
0.97	1/6	0.249
0.84	1/5	0.280
0.67	1/4	0.319
0.43	1/3	0.364
0.00	1/2	0.399
−0.43	2/3	0.364
−0.67	3/4	0.319
−0.84	4/5	0.280
−1.29	9/10	0.174
−2.32	99/100	0.027

Expectancy tables

Correlation	Selection ratio			
	0.2	0.4	0.6	0.8
Per cent satisfactory acceptees if **30%** of applicants satisfactory				
0.15	38	35	33	32
0.2	40	37	34	32
0.3	46	40	37	33
0.4	51	44	39	34
0.5	58	48	41	35
0.6	64	52	43	36
0.7	72	57	46	37
Per cent satisfactory acceptees if **40%** of applicants satisfactory				
0.15	48	46	44	42
0.2	51	48	45	43
0.3	57	51	47	44
0.4	63	56	50	45
0.5	69	60	53	46
0.6	75	64	55	48
0.7	82	69	58	49
Per cent satisfactory acceptees if **50%** of applicants satisfactory				
0.15	58	56	54	52
0.2	61	58	55	53
0.3	67	62	58	54
0.4	73	66	61	56
0.5	78	70	63	57
0.6	84	75	66	59
0.7	90	80	70	60
Per cent satisfactory acceptees if **60%** of applicants satisfactory				
0.15	68	66	64	62
0.2	71	71	68	64
0.3	76	71	68	64
0.4	81	75	70	66
0.5	86	79	73	67
0.6	90	83	76	69
0.7	94	87	80	71
Per cent satisfactory acceptees if **70%** of applicants satisfactory				
0.15	77	75	73	72
0.2	79	77	75	73
0.3	84	80	77	74
0.4	88	83	79	75
0.5	91	87	82	77
0.6	95	90	85	79
0.7	97	93	88	80

References

Arnold, J. D., Rauschenberger, J. M, Soubel, W. G. and Guion, R. M. (1982) 'Validation and utility of a strength test for selecting steel workers', *Journal of Applied Psychology*, 67, **5**, 588–604.

Boudreau, J. W. (1983) 'Economic considerations in the utility of human resource programs', *Personnel Psychology*, 36, 551–76.

Boudreau, J. W. and Rynes, S. L. (1985) 'Role of recruitment in staffing utility analysis', *Journal of Applied Psychology*, 70, **2**, 354–66.

Cascio, W. F. and Silbey, V. (1979) 'Utility of the assessment center as a selection device', *Journal of Applied Psychology*, 64, 107–18.

Lee, R. and Booth, J. M. (1974) 'A utility analysis of a weighted application blank designed to predict turnover for clerical employees', *Journal of Applied Psychology*, 59, **4**, 516–518.

Schmidt, F. L., Hunter, J. E., McKenzie, R. C. and Muldrow, T. W. (1979) 'Impact of valid selection procedures on workforce productivity', *Journal of Applied Psychology*, 64, **6**, 609–26.

10 Issues from a practitioner's standpoint

Why improve?

Tom Peters says 'If it ain't broke, you aren't looking hard enough'. And the selection and assessment of staff can certainly do with periodic and searching review. All personnel staff are aware of the improvement in presentation and motivation of senior candidates in being interviewed. Several books and outplacement consultancies have worked towards giving applicants skills in answering leadership questions and even in dealing with tests. William Whyte's *Organisation Man* started the trend in applicant tuition some years ago.

The personal biases of an interviewer in a company are usually submerged or latent. It is often difficult to assess the true reasons for a candidate's rejection since line managers learn that he or she must not express personal prejudice.

With fuller employment, organisations are also forced to turn to less obvious sources of recruitment or to the previously unconsidered candidates from traditional sources. Help and experience are needed to ascertain if the recently retired older person or the returning-to-work mother has the motivation, ability and attitude to succeed or whether the arts graduate has the necessary ingredients to follow a technological career despite his or her secondary and tertiary education preferences. Even the most obvious sources of candidates are not easy to assess – school leavers, designers and research graduates are examples of people whose lack of experience or exposure to different value systems makes it difficult for a personnel manager, let alone a line manager, to evaluate the likelihood of career success. Experience with school teachers wanting to work in industry has tested the author's own skills in judging people's ability to succeed in a change of career.

But the more mundane and straightforward pressures on reviewing selection practices come from the benefits of promoting the right people from within. Apart from the good personnel practice of doing this and the reduction of induction time, the costs and uncertainties of appointing from outside, with consultant's fees up from 15 per cent of salaries twenty years ago to 33.3 per cent or more now, gives an economic imperative to internal promotion.

The last concern comes in an organisation which cannot, because of geography or other reasons, carry out centralised recruitment. Hotels and retail chains are obvious examples of the need to delegate recruitment or selection from London or any other large metropolis to line managers in, for example, Penzance or Arbroath. Standards must be met but the temptation of a line manager under pressure is often to go for the first candidate or those with the 'warmest bodies'. The most used selection and assessment tool is the interview, which needs to be rigidly standardised and made uniform to enable consistent measurements to be made. The interview's attraction for decentralising recruitment and maintaining standards is obvious.

Where to improve

The question of where to review selection and assessment procedures in an organisation is obviously dependent on the organisation itself. There are really only three places to start – at the top, at the level where many similar candidates are hired, or where there is one job with many incumbents.

The best place to introduce the benefits of modern assessment techniques is obviously at the top of a company. Here recruitment is crucial. A mistake at this level causes damage in profits, costs and morale, quite apart from being visible and holding top management up to some unjust ridicule at being unable to pick the right person. Using assessment consultants as an extra step in the recruiting process is valuable for several reasons. It is never wrong to make any organisation difficult to get into – it shows the importance of standards as well as being an insurance policy against mistakes for both the company and the applicant. Using an independent assessor is easily justifiable. It is another useful viewpoint to be considered and where internal candidates are being compared with external applicants, the less biased the opinions that can be offered the better. This usage of assessors is now relatively conventional among most organisations and can form the stepping stone for convincing management that similar systematic processes can be used elsewhere in the company.

However, the benefits of economy alone must lead an organisation to consider objective selection systems for discriminating between large numbers of similar applicants, especially school leavers and graduates, who in the latter case are being hired both for their future potential as well as for an immediate job.

Similarly, objective assessment is necessary where applicants from diverse backgrounds apply for a job with many incumbents. For example, with salespeople, secretaries, engineers, and foreign exchange dealers, it is necessary to analyse beforehand the constituents for success in such positions and to establish how these constituents will be elicited and compared.

The most usual preconditions for reviewing and improving selection and assessment methods can be summarised as follows:

- bad experience(s) with traditional methods;
- growing recruiting costs;
- increasing turnover of staff, especially in the early days of service which indicates at least an induction problem but more probably poor recruiting procedures;
- a shortage of 'traditional' applicants;
- the CRE or EOC indicating possible discriminatory practices towards what many in society consider minorities in the working population.

Making it happen

Once the decision to review practices has been made and the most beneficial or necessary area identified, the next steps (though not all are necessary) are usually as follows.

- Find a senior line manager or director who will champion the analytical approach to recruitment. An 'umbrella' man or woman is nearly always indispensable whenever piloting anything that is new.
- Calculate the costs involved in the current practices and list the failures and shortcomings already experienced.
- Search for any previous success in 'unusual' or non-traditional hires who challenge current wisdom and who may have been appointed because someone had belief in them. The author particularly remembers appointing a lorry driver who had the right characteristics and who is now a highly successful manager. This helped to break the company's traditional approach and encouraged the company to look for candidates from quite diverse backgrounds.
- Suggest a pilot study in a limited area. Trying to change everyone on one experiment is fraught with risks and difficulties.
- Know quite clearly before the start what is wanted from the experiment and establish what all will agree is success or failure from this test. Concentration then must be focused on the means to those ends. Unclear ends will open a Pandora's box of troubles and expose the organisation to hiring mavericks who are peddling packages.

Do it yourself or finding consultants

All the techniques listed in this book require some degree of specialist and even statistical or computing expertise. There is the possibility of using an in-house psychologist if the size of organisation warrants such a position. The problem here though is often the credibility of such a person elsewhere in the organisation. Certainly an in-house expert is going to be cheaper and could certainly handle the lower level jobs. But top level assessment by a staff member is usually not acceptable to candidates above the level of that professional, or to top management themselves. Further, the methods or techniques now emerging make it unlikely, but not impossible, for the company expert to be *au fait* with the latest developments or able to devise the necessary norms to validate approaches within the confines of an average sized organisation. Moreover, many techniques now require access to specialist software which is often the preserve of the consultant who has developed it. Consultants or academics should be unbiased, especially if not tied in financially to recruiting organisations, and should have experience in other concerns and companies. They are a cost-effective way to give the necessary short-term injection of expertise and can then be dispensed with afterwards.

Whichever course – consultant or in-house professional – is chosen, the experts must have the necessary experience and rapport with the relevant levels and ages within the company. Young outplacement consultants who have never been made redundant, for example, must raise questions of appropriateness. This also applies to assessment consultants who have rarely mingled with top management.

Furthermore, one must also be clear about what will be a successful conclusion of the assignment. How long will the tool or procedure be required and who will be able or unable to use it within the company in future? A person within the company may need to be trained to ensure the effective maintenance of the programme.

Finding such experts is difficult. Reading professional and technical journals, attending relevant conferences and seminars, asking friends or even competitors in one's sector are all tried methods. Making enquiries through the Institute of Personnel Management or British Psychological Society, as well as keeping mailshots, tiresome though it may be, will often yield results.

Selecting consultants

Selecting the appropriate adviser follows similar rules to those for choosing consultants for other assignments. Suggested guidelines are:

- Determine how wide the scope or the number of jobs you wish to cover. Short-staged assignments are better than a fully comprehensive coverage of a whole tier of a company.
- Write your brief as fully as possible and stick to it unless you are later convinced of the need for a modification.
- Set how much money and time you have available and are prepared to devote to the operation.
- Decide how closely involved you wish to be. Is there a preference for a fully devised selection procedure or is it desirable for company involvement at various stages?
- Consider who else in the organisation should be involved in the briefing and selection of the approach and the consultants.

Then evaluate the two or three consultants you have approached or short-listed along the following criteria:

- Do they listen to your needs rather than present their research or fixed ideas?
- Have they done something similar before and for whom? They do not necessarily need to have worked in your business but certainly in an organisation of similar culture and values.
- Do they repeat and confirm, to your satisfaction, what you are looking for?
- What is the quality of their written and their oral presentation? It is far too common for PhDs or even senior lecturers to be illiterate and ungrammatical!
- What is the pedigree of the people? The organisation to which they belong is irrelevant: one is hiring people, not a company.
- Is it a one-man band or a company? Are there enough competent people to cover? Big companies quite fallaciously

prefer to use big companies or big names, and an eminent person might be supported only by assistants or research students.

- Do they carefully but firmly disagree with some of your ideas or steps? This may well be a good sign of their competence.
- Establish how well the advisers can explain their approach. A simple test would be to ask for an explanation of what a repertory grid is or how cluster analysis works. Advisers can too easily become involved in the theoretical and academic aspects of work and leave the company feeling that modern alchemists are at hand.
- Is there a subordinate or colleague in the consultant organisation (or your own company) who is pushing for a specific approach or technique to complete his or her knowledge without regard to the real problem?
- Do you like them and feel at ease with them? If your chief executive or shop steward suddenly walked into the room, would you feel the need to apologise for them?

Costs Justification

The matter of how much to spend is difficult to calculate precisely. The organisation's budgetary constraints are one aspect but to evaluate whether there is a case, a compilation of all the costs of recruitment and staff turnover need to be quantified. This should include an estimation of the time currently spent assessing candidates. More relevantly, one should collect evidence on the costs and impact of bad appointment decisions. The author has kept a log of all selection decisions, segregating them into good and bad with details on why the unsatisfactory candidate was chosen. It is also good practice to note where appointments were made against one's recommendations and to establish the outcome.

Certainly any potential adviser should be asked for a detailed cost breakdown of their tender, which should include expenses. The project likewise should be split into parts so that negotiations can be over discrete areas. The programme will inevitably change, thus making renegotiations easier. The lure of further work, especially in expanding a pilot to the whole organisation, will ensure keen pricing. Enquiries as to the adviser's current and future workload and alternative starting dates may lead to an agreement that is convenient and cheaper. Certainly, explaining what needs to be done by consultants and what can be done by one's own staff has also yielded both useful savings and increased staff competence.

Managing consultants

Managing the study requires regular meetings. 'No surprises' must be the catch-phrase and the client needs to follow and understand each step of the programme. Packages must not be thrown at the problem because each organisation is unique and needs tailor-made solutions.

Many findings or steps may challenge conventional wisdom. Thorough comprehension is necessary and each finding must have some face validity or be explicable by common sense. In this scientific age, one's colleagues will critique every detail of a new departure and will find many justifications or loopholes to satisfy their scepticism.

Detailed periodical debates with the advisers are essential. Psychometrics is an imprecise science despite, for instance, the manuals of statistical validity and reliability which can bestow some theoretical renown upon tests. It is often surprising when debating a consultant's findings how far the interpretation can be modified. A case in point was a consultant's comment that a candidate lacked energy. Queries were raised as to which tests and evidence led to that conclusion. The result was that 'in some circumstances, he lacked energy'. Suffice to say the candidate was later fired for taking on far too much and rushing around like a maniac. The anecdote is meant to prove nothing except that even an amateur collecting his or her information has as valid a view point as an expert on occasions and should not be overawed.

Another area to be watched is the problem of bias. On some initial constructs it can be that women or members of ethnic groups do score differently and sometimes significantly so. One has to insist on further analysis. Perhaps it was the sample – insufficient or skewed; perhaps some elements of the job were not as relevant as originally though, or perhaps in the interests of fairness some of the discriminatory test elements can be discarded and reliance placed on other factors which do not show a sex, race or age bias.

Lastly, where a study involves the eliciting of competencies, usually for senior levels, the organisation must insist on its own competencies being defined and not those that fit some national prediction or consensus or academic research. There are many who would force us into categories that nearly fit. Rely on your own observations and argue tenaciously before you agree. The world is full of species, hybrids and varities; categorisation increases the scientist's ability to understand but it does not naturally increase the well-being of the particular species under study.

Making it transplant

There are a number of caveats to bear in mind both during and after the study for a successful introduction.

- An organisation basically wants an ability to judge and assess, not test. Judgment by definition is not accurate; it is an interplay of many factors and conclusions based on probabilities. There is no perfect assessment tool. Without wanting to go into theological waters, even Christ picked Judas Iscariot.
- Make sure the criteria in any assessment system reflect current *and* future changes at work. Otherwise the system will pick yesterday's people with today's systems. Selection methods can only operate on the model defined. What factors, traits and attributes will be necessary for tomorrow's jobs? Concentration on today's model raises the danger of defining the best and worst performers in today's environment: they may not be the best or worst tomorrow.
- Ensure your own staff learn how to operate the schemes and validate them over time. The client is not buying a black box; the organisation has to be able to maintain and adapt the techniques in the future. A psychologist is a design

engineer; their clients must be production engineers.

- Profiling and assessment centres frequently identify unexpected people to be the new bosses. This often surprises users. It is not just the theory that the best salesman is unlikely to be the best sales manager. The next generation of managers may have diametrically different skills, values *and* expertise from those emphasised by existing managers. In the United States health facility management is no longer the preserve of a doctor or a surgeon. The head of a health facility is now hopefully someone who is able to set the attitudes and practices that let other people do the job of health care and is a separate career with only moderate medical training.
- Another key point, curiously but perhaps not unexpectedly ignored by psychologists, is test fatigue. Two or three hours of taking tests and even personality profiles, can and does make an average person very tired and perhaps careless. This may produce a 'near enough is good enough' approach in an applicant, which may obscure their potential. Modern life is full of questionnaires from market research to intelligence tests and many people get frustrated and irritated at answering other people's questions without the facility to challenge the obvious underlying assumptions of a test set.
- Assessment centres take up much time and are, at root, role plays. Do all assessment centre candidates feel real-life adrenalin in such a fabricated situation and perform at their best?
- The power of modern assessment techniques has caused what might be called the Pygmalion effect. A few senior managers now determine their attitudes to staff by their staff's results in assessment centres and selection tests. As an example the author recalls a reasonably average performer who was regarded as substandard by her superior. When the woman was assessed, it was shown to her boss that her intelligence test results were very high and that her personality for the job was more than adequate. As a result she was regarded and treated as a star, which she patently was not. It took a further twelve months to

get him to balance his judgement because he believed tests were infallible and scientific.

- The company must evaluate before implementing new selection procedures whether:
  - the testing methods require too much of the individual and of the time and money resources of the company;
  - any in-company assessors fall back into judging the whole person rather than assessing the individual criteria being evaluated at each stage;
  - there is enough use of new technologies, for example, interviews and group meetings could be conducted on video without the presence of observers. This is useful insofar as re-runs could be called for when points of difference between observers need verification.
- A last concern is that far too frequently any assessment techniques are regarded by candidates as pass or fail. It will need consistent disclaimers to the contrary and the building-in of professional debriefing and the construction of personal development plans to counteract this belief. Life is about success or failure but candidates often fail to make the graduations between the extremes. Even making the programme a universal experience may only mitigate the dissatisfaction of not being promoted. On the other hand, a far more insidious problem is the individual who is awakened to and then confirmed of his or her potential only to find that there are no vacancies available in the necessary timespan.

These problems are for overcoming, not for deferring or abandoning the introduction of more systematic assessment techniques. Their success is proven and can yield a competitive edge in better appointment or use of human resources. The problems are an indication of how hard the personnel function has to work to ensure a successful implementation and to avoid the excesses of the sceptic or the fanatic.

Other benefits

Lest the various caveats seem daunting, it is appropriate to enumerate the additional benefits and ways of improving the calibre of staff that can be achieved through introducing systematic selection.

The analysis of managerial competencies can form the basis for all selection. It is a clearly articulated set of standards that in turn can be converted into structured interviews and a series of relevant tests. Further, the competencies are valuable in more clearly forming the culture of the organisation or 'the way managers do things here'. These lists of competencies have been used in describing the mission statement of an organisation and lend to that statement a flavour that objectives themselves cannot give.

Competencies can also be used to develop and train staff and then form part of the appraisal and potential identification process. Job redesign can also be an output of the analysis of competencies. The results may make all too clear the fact that some levels or roles force people to act and behave in conflicting ways. The job may force its holder into a 'no win' position. This may be an underlying reason for staff turnover, as staff are unable to perform adequately when job demands conflict or contradict each other.

A thorough understanding of what is needed at any level, and how it meshes with the levels above and below can help more rapid culture change to adapt to commercial needs. While job analysis and *systematic* assessment suggest rigidity, the data and process can enhance evolution. Companies tend to change slowly and painfully, rather than alter by revolution. So, often it is useful for this process to establish the current situation in terms of what each job level does and how it does it. With this knowledge, jobs and people can be adapted, modified and developed. Without it, any attempts to change will be stabs in the dark, too difficult and too unreliable perhaps even to be attempted.

Improvements and cost savings can also be gained by extending the work done in one area into another. Very often the analysis of competencies can be adapted to suit another related area. The assessment and selection techniques may also be appropriate. It is wise to validate them on the new group but it is often not necessary to go through the whole process again. This provides obvious savings; it also yields cost benefits if the new procedures improve the calibre of this related group. Similarly, it may be that the new selection procedures could be extended using the same initial analysis. If, for example, a job analysis has produced an assessment centre for graduates, perhaps the same analysis could be used to design a screening system or even to improve the quality of the advertisement.

Reviewing and improving assessment methods is an essential task facing today's personnel function. The phenomenal changes in the nature of work and the market-place over the last ten years demands that attention be directed towards improving the calibre of all new joiners and towards identifying and developing talent in current staff.

The task itself, whilst perhaps appearing at first glance to be daunting as there are numerous pitfalls for the unwary, is undoubtedly beneficial. Immediate and specific benefits pertain to the job or level investigated, and extensions of the data and process within that group or to other similar job categories produce improvements and cost savings. Longer term benefits pertain where the data is used to assist culture change or 'humanise' mission statements.

11 Deselection and outplacement

Deselection as a part of human resource management

Until quite recently, many personnel specialists saw selection only in terms of recruitment *into* an organisation – the input of employees to an organisational system. This simplistic view assumes that organisations either continue to grow or at best remain static. Events of the early 1980s gave decisive evidence that this view is wrong. There are times when organisations need to contract. There are also times when an organisation needs to change the composition of its workforce quite dramatically. Obvious examples spring to mind. Due to the collapse in oil prices and increased competition from imports the British coal industry was forced to shrink its workforce quite dramatically over the space of just a few years. Similarly, when the old electro-mechanical telephone exchanges were replaced by electronic exchanges, telephone companies around the world found that their workforces had obsolescent 'look, hear and poke' skills, which could be exercised in a group situation and where a mistake would have consequences over a relatively small area. The new electronic exchanges required abstract analytic skills exercised in a solitary situation and where a mistake would wipe out communications across a whole city. Furthermore, the new exchanges were more reliable and needed fewer staff to maintain them. Technological change had rendered void a whole generation of effort in training and selection.

Classic outplacement situations of this kind need to be managed as efficiently as the classic recruitment situations. Indeed, from a human resource viewpoint they pose a greater challenge. Often, outplacement situations occur without much warning and they can mean dealing with thousands of people within a very short time. In addition, emotions are usually running very high. Under these circumstances, it is little wonder that many outplacement situations are not managed as effectively as possible.

Consequences of badly managed outplacement

In essence, the consequence of a badly managed outplacement situation is that the quality of the remaining workforce is diminished. This is ironic. Situations involving the reduction of a workforce usually occur when organisations are facing difficulties or threats – the very time when a workforce of the highest quality is needed. The reduction in the quality of the workforce happens in two main ways: deselection of the wrong people and the effect on the morale of those who remain.

Deselection of the wrong people

There is a growing body of evidence that in a redundancy situation, organisations divest themselves of people of above average ability. For example, Coutts Career Consultants conducted an analysis of a sample of over 200 managers who had been declared redundant. On the basis of the results from standardised, objective psychological tests, it was found that redundant managers were more:

- *intelligent:* the average manager in the sample had an IQ of 129 compared with an average of 123 for managers who were attending courses at a major UK business school;
- *venturesome* and willing to take risks: even in difficult social situations these men were likely to remain communicative and fluent;
- *stable, calm, confident and relaxed:* they were unlikely to over-react in an emergency and they had the stamina and resilience to rise above difficult situations. However, in the

eyes of neurotic and over-anxious superiors they would appear to be complacent;
- *independent:* they tended to be assertive and imaginative. This means that they were prepared to take responsibility and push proposals through. They would be able to see beyond the obvious possibilities and so their work would have a degree of imagination and flair;
- *experienced:* the managers made redundant were rather above average in terms of experience – especially experience in production, collecting information and solving problems.

Similar conclusions have been produced by two other studies which were conducted at different times in different settings. The implications for an organisation are quite dramatic and can be best illustrated with a hypothetical example of an organisation which intends to reduce a cadre of middle management from 150 to 50. If the average salary is 50,000 ecus per year and the average tenure of the retained managers is four years, the techniques outlined in Chapter 9 can be used to estimate, from the intelligence tests alone, that the mismanagement of the outplacement of these managers would cost approximately 848,000 ecus over the four-year period – not counting the effects of inflation and tax.

The question arises, why do organisations exercise such self flagellation in times of great need? There appear to be three possible answers: redundancy procedures; the grit in the oyster hypothesis; and the talent blindness hypothesis.

In times of redundancy it is almost universal to operate *procedures of voluntary redundancy* and if this fails to produce sufficient reduction in staffing levels, there is then a *procedure of last in first out*. Both procedures could act as a selective filter. There is little empirical research to act as an authoritative guide but it is plausible to argue that in a voluntary redundancy situation those who volunteer tend to be the talented employees who have little difficulty in obtaining alternative work. It is also possible to envisage that in last in, first out situations the employees that remain are the rump of a group of employees engaged many years ago and that the most able of their cohort have either been promoted or had the initiative to obtain advancement elsewhere.

The second mechanism leading organisations to lose their most talented employees can be termed the *grit in the oyster hypothesis*. It argues that in most organisations there are individuals who do not totally accept the status quo and who question assumptions and methods. In normal times these individuals act as a benign irritant who spur the organisation on to better things in much the same way that a small piece of grit induces an oyster to produce a pearl. In normal times these individuals will be tolerated and even encouraged, but in difficult times the organisation adopts a defensive posture and draws in its horns.

The third reason why organisations might divest themselves of the most talented people is *an inability to recognise talent*. Often this inability can occur for quite banal reasons. For example, one company had embarked on a contraction of a management grade from 1,300 to 35. It first operated a policy of voluntary redundancy which reduced the number of contenders for the 35 posts to about 500. Due partly to union pressure it then decided that the allocation of the 35 posts should be based on individual merit. The question arose, how could this individual merit be assessed? Most organisations would probably rely on recommendations from superiors, but fortunately for at least one individual the company decided to supplement this information with results from a series of tests. The results from the tests suggested that the individual had first rate potential whilst the report from his superior indicated a mediocre performer without any real advantages or disadvantages. The discrepancy was so great that checks were made on both sets of information and it emerged that due to domestic circumstances the man concerned had managed the night shift for several years while his superior had managed the day shift. The two rarely met and the superior had little knowledge of the man; consequently he filed an acceptable, middle of the road report which was in fact a travesty and which nearly cost his subordinate a job.

In this particular example the inability to recognise talent was due to operational reasons but sometimes it can also arise from malevolent causes: times of redundancy offer excellent opportunities to settle old scores or remove threats posed by able subordinates.

The effects on morale

Another way in which outplacement can degrade the quality of a workforce is to reduce morale and motivation so that employees are less keen and willing to perform their work. Demotivation can occur in two ways: the demotivation of those deselected and the demotivation of those who remain.

The demotivation of those who leave is more important than it first appears. From an ethical viewpoint, many organisations care about the future well-being of those who may have given loyal service over many years. Consequently many employers have a sincere wish, often backed by real resources, to make the transition of those who are deselected as painless as possible and that outplaced employees will retain dignity and new employment which offers job satisfaction. Often, it is also in the organisation's self-interest to maintain the morale of deselected employees. Usually there is a considerable time lapse between the announcement of deselection and the employee actually leaving the organisation. It is highly desirable that the employee remains effective during this period. The problem is particularly acute at senior levels who may be the first to know of a redundancy programme but who may be retained until the last moment in order to manage it. Difficult situations of this kind are not helped by the fact that the manager's attention may be divided between the time-consuming activity of managing other people's redundancy on behalf of the organisation and the chores of finding re-employment for themselves.

The complete closure of an organisation is quite rare. Therefore *the motivation of those who remain* is usually the largest problem of morale. The danger is that once the relief of being spared has worn off, the staff who are retained become bitter and defensive. They may come to the conclusions that there were no justifiable reasons for the redundancies and that staff lost their jobs on a random or malevolent basis. Perhaps the most damaging belief is that the organisation is exploitative and discards employees without help or remorse when they no longer required. Staff who come to hold such beliefs are not likely to give long term commitment to an organisation. Instead, they may become defensive and withhold information and knowledge in the belief that it makes them less dispensable and less vulnerable to any future wave of outplacement. In reality the opposite is often true. A wide-scale collapse of team spirit can reduce efficiency, exacerbate an already difficult situation and bring about further job losses – the main victims of which are those individuals who are considered to be inflexible and uncooperative.

The role of selection and assessment in outplacement

Selection and assessment procedures have three main roles to play in an outplacement situation: establishing future skill requirements, guiding the retention of the most able employees and giving appropriate career advice to those who leave.

The outplacement of some employees is almost invariably accompanied by a reorganisation of those who remain. The reorganised jobs may involve new skills or a different mix of skills. Effective management of an outplacement situation cannot be accomplished without *establishing future skill requirements*. Sometimes the techniques of job and skill analysis outlined in Chapter 2 can be used to achieve this aim – this is especially true when the reorganisation involves a recombination of the components of existing jobs. It may even be possible to establish future skill requirements by amending existing job descriptions.

In more extreme situations, totally new jobs are created and existing sources of information cannot be used. Probably the only method which can be used in this type of situation is the 'technical conference' method in which a group of experts meet to decide upon the likely skill requirements. Unfortunately, the opinions of experts are often subjective. Fortunately, only broad brush conclusions are needed at this point. Often, all that is needed is a list of the five or six main skills which will be needed to perform the new job. In many cases the overriding requirements are the intelligence and flexibility to be able to adapt quickly to new circumstances.

A whole panoply of methods can be used to guide companies in *retaining the most talented employees*. Most of the methods described elsewhere in this book could be used. One of the biggest problems is to organise a cost-effective system which is understood and acceptable to all concerned.

One particular combination starts with a superior's recommendation. Those who are recommended to be retained are then asked to participate in some central procedure which usually involves an assessment centre containing several work-sample exercises. This combination suffers three large disadvantages. First, it is based on superiors' recommendations and it is known that these recommendations are not very accurate. Inaccuracy at the start of a procedure inevitably limits the accuracy of the system as a whole. Second, the system may be very unfair. At its most blatant it offers the superior the chance to settle old scores with those who in the past have pointed out his shortcomings. Slightly less objectionably, different superiors have different standards of judgement and it is a matter of luck whether someone is working for a 'hard' superior or an 'easy' one. Systems in which superiors' opinions play a dominant role are often perceived, rightly or wrongly, as being unfair. Third, a system of this kind may be prohibitively expensive. Assessment centres are very resource intensive and in an attempt to counter claims of subjectivity superiors may be lenient in forwarding the names of marginal employees.

An alternative system involves three stages: asking for volunteers; psychological tests; and assessment centres.

The first voluntary stage usually finds wide acceptance from the current workforce and their representatives. The second stage is objective and will be seen to be fair since the testing is usually done by an outside organisation with no vested interests towards specific individuals and little knowledge of past conflicts or animosities. Furthermore, test scores are less contaminated than many methods by such factors as social background, accent, school attended and, as we have seen in Chapter 9, by race, sex or age. The tests used should be well standardised and, above all else, relevant to the skills needed in the reconstructed job. An advantage of using tests as a second stage filter is that they are relatively cheap to administer and, indeed, the unit cost falls quite dramatically as the numbers of people tested increase. The savings in cost can be reinvested in the final stage – assessment centres. Usually, the assessment centres are of one or two-day duration and at least some of the assessors should be disinterested parties – preferably from an outside organisation.

Career counselling and outplacement

All deselection programmes have an enormous influence on the personal lives of the employees who are deselected. It is callous for organisations to discard employees without making proper provision to enable them to find new jobs and readjust to new situations. Often employers fall into the trap of believing that a large financial provision of redundancy pay is an adequate response to a distressing human situation. Large sums of redundancy pay are often accompanies by large tax demands. Often, the greatest need is for counselling and advice. Probably the most longstanding and loyal ex-employees have not applied for a job for several decades and, furthermore, they have experienced the greatest shock. There is a moral obligation on employers to meet these needs either from resources within the organisation or by buying in external resources.

For example, one large organisation in the communication industry anticipated the need for a deselection programme for several hundred staff. It then commissioned its training department to develop a two-week course in which local personnel professionals were given the skills and the knowledge to counsel the individuals affected. Only then did the outplacement programme commence. The effect of this strategy was to reduce the emotional trauma on those whose jobs were declared redundant. It also reduced the trauma for members of the personnel function. Previously most personnel staff were conducting difficult, unpredictable and time-consuming counselling sessions for which they had received no training. Often the sessions were doomed to failure and the failure reduced morale in a situation where morale was already low. The establishment of a cadre of redundancy counsellors meant that others could get on with the vital task of efficiently managing the personnel function and morale was given some support by the greater success rate of the counselling sessions.

Smaller organisations may not have either the resources or expertise to follow such a strategy and may need to engage the services of an outplacement organisation which normally include the following.

- *Career counselling* where, perhaps with the aid of the results from psychological tests, an employee is encouraged to take stock of his past career and develop a future career direction.
- *Job search* to help the individual locate vacancies which meet their requirements. At senior levels this may involve the employment of a researcher to scan a wide range of publications for adverts and to identify those organisations which seem likely to need the executive's particular blend of skills. At more junior levels in a large outplacement situation help with the job search may involve establishing a 'job shop' within the organisation's premises where employees can call in on a casual basis, ask for help with applications or browse through files of vacancies.
- *CV preparation* can range from merely offering advice on the contents and style of a curriculum vitae to a full secretarial service which manages the production of CVs and 'mailshots' of speculative applications.

In addition, a full outplacement service will offer investment advice in respect of lump sum redundancy payments and closed circuit television training in interview techniques.

Whether these services are provided on an internal or external basis, probably the most important component is that it is clear that the employee is not being simply cast aside. This helps the outplaced employee adjust to the situation and it also helps the remaining employees maintain their regard and loyalty to their employer.

Further reading

Very little written material on the outplacement function is available – either from the UK or even the USA where the outplacement function is quite well developed.

Information on the characteristics of managers who have been made redundant is available in:

Hartley, J. F. (1980) 'The impact of unemployment on the self-esteem of managers', *Journal of Occupational Psychology*, 53, 147–55.

Smith, J. M. (1989) *'The paradox of talent'*, occasional research paper, Coutts Career Consultants, 11 Whitehall, London.

A practical book of help to individual outplaced employees is:

Nathan, R. and Syrett, M. (1981) *How to Survive Redundancy*, London, Institute of Personnel Management.

Name and organisation index

Subject index